P9-CBP-851

Devotion:
Loving God

THE mananam SERIES

(Mananam–Sanskrit for "Reflection upon the Truth")

(continued on inside back page)

THE mananamSERIES

Devotion:
Loving God

CHINMAYA PUBLICATIONS
CHINMAYA MISSION WEST PUBLICATIONS DIVISION

Chinmaya Publications
Chinmaya Mission West Publications Division

P.O. Box 129
Piercy, CA 95587, USA

Distribution Office
560 Bridgetowne Pike
Langhorne, PA 19053
Phone: (215) 396-0390   Fax: (215) 396-9710
Toll Free: 1-888-CMW-READ (1-888-269-7323)
Internet: www.mananam.org
          www.chinmayapublications.org

Central Chinmaya Mission Trust
Sandeepany Sadhanalaya
Saki Vihar Road
Mumbai, India 400 072

Copyright 2003 by Chinmaya Mission West.
All rights reserved. Published 2003.
Permission to reprint may be granted on request to:
Editor, editor@mananam.org
Printed in the United States of America.

Credits:
Editorial Advisor: Swami Shantananda
Series Editors: Margaret Leuverink, Rashmi Mehrotra
Associate Editor: Neena Dev
Editorial Assistants: Swamini Shivapriyananda, Pat Loganathan,
                 Vinni Soni
Cover Photograph: Swami Siddhananda
Cover Graphics and Inside Illustrations: Christine Wong, Neena Dev
Production Manager: Arun Mehrotra

Library of Congress Catalog Card Number: 2003103727
ISBN 1-880687-54-2

Previously published and copyrighted materials reprinted with the kind permission of the authors, publishers or copyright owners as listed below:

Beckwith, Rev. Michael. *For the Love of God.* © 1997 by Benjamin Shield and Richard Carlson. Reprinted by permission of New World Library, 14 Pamaron Way, Novato, CA 94949.

Daya Mata, Sri. *Finding the Joy Within You: Personal Counsel for God-Centered Living.* © 1990 by Sri Daya Mata. Reprinted by permission of Self-Realization Fellowship, 3880 San Rafael Avenue, Los Angeles, California 90065.

Frawley, David. *Vedantic Meditation.* © 2000 by David Frawley. Reprinted by permission of the author, www.vedanet.com.

Kearney, Tim. *A Prophetic Cry.* © 2000 by Jean Vanier. Reprinted by permission of Veritas Publications, 718 Lower Abbey Street, Dublin 1, Dublin.

Khan, Hazrat Inayat. *The Sufi Message of Hazrat Inayat Khan* Volume 5. © 1962 by Hazrat Inayat Khan. Reprinted by permission of International Headquarters of the Sufi Movement, Den Haag, Netherlands.

Powell, Father John. *Unconditional Love.* © 1978, 1999 by John Powell, SJ. Reprinted by permission of Thomas More Publishing, 200 West Bethany Drive, Allen, Texas 75002.

Rinpoche, Sogyal. *The Tibetan Book of Living and Dying.* © 1993 by Sogyal Rinpoche. Reprinted by permission of Harper Collins Publishers, 10 East 53rd. Street, New York, NY 10022-5299.

Swami Ashokananda. *Ascent to Spiritual Illumination.* © 2001 by Advaita Ashram. Reprinted by permission of Advaita Ashram, Mayawati, Champawat, Himalayas, India.

Swami Budhananda. *Vedanta and the West.* Reprinted by permission of Vedanta Society of Southern California, Hollywood, CA 90068.

Swami Pramathananda. *The Vedanta Kesari, July 2002.* Reprinted by permission of The Vedanta Kesari, Ramakrishna Math, No. 31, Ramakrishna Math Road, Mylapore, Chennai, 600 004, India.

Swami Ramdas. *Ramdas Speaks* Volume IV. © 1971 by Swami Ramdas. Reprinted by permission of Bharatiya Vidya Bhavan, Munshi Sadan, Kulpati K. M. Munshi Marg, Mumbai 400 007, India

Swami Shraddhananda. *The Vedanta Kesari.* Reprinted by permission of The Vedanta Kesari, Ramakrishna Math, No. 31, Ramakrishna Math Road, Mylapore, Chennai, 600 004, India.

Swami Swahananda. *Meditation and Other Spiritual Disciplines.* © 1983 by Advaita Ashram. Reprinted by permission of Advaita Ashram, Mayawati, Chapawat, Himalayas, India.

Swami Viprananda. *The Vedanta Kesari.* Reprinted by permission of The Vedanta Kesari, Ramakrishna Math, No. 31 Ramakrishna Math Road, Mylapore, Chennai, 600 004, India.

Swami Yatiswarananda. *Meditation and Spiritual Life.* © 1983 by Sri Ramakrishna Ashram. Reprinted by permission of Sri Ramakrishna Ashram, Bull Temple Rd., Bangalore 560 019, India.

Contents

PART THREE

SURRENDER UNTO HIM

Preface

Nothing in the world is more powerful than love. The noblest kind of love is the kind that flows towards God, which is called devotion. Saints and sages affirm that deep within our heart lies an infinite source of love, with no beginning and no end. While loving people, ideas, and objects we are in fact, endlessly searching for this infinite love. How to cultivate devotion, so that we can rediscover the permanent source of love and bliss within ourselves, is the topic of this book.

Part One describes the nature of devotion. We are most familiar with love for things and beings around us but that love, being limited, cannot satisfy us for long. However devotion—love of God—leads to a greater and more expansive vision of life that brings total fulfillment.

Cultivating divine virtues such as kindness and compassion brings us closer to God and helps our love for Him to grow. This is the topic of Part Two. In this section the authors describe the importance of prayer, faith, meditation, repetition of the Lord's name, and selfless service. Devotional practices, when performed with sincerity, purify the mind and we thus come to radiate love and goodwill to all.

The ultimate in the development of devotion is surrender, which is the topic of Part Three. The authors indicate that continuous remembrance of God and realization that He is the One doing everything, and that everything comes from Him, constitutes surrender. Stories of great devotees inspire us to greater heights and strengthen our faith. It is the intensity of love and faith that help us surrender and we begin to listen to the Divine voice of love within our hearts.

Through devotion we are led to that most sacred place, the Self, the Source of all love and compassion. When we direct our love toward the higher our vision expands and we see the Divine everywhere, in everyone, and in everything. Thus we come to love everyone and all of creation equally, enjoying lasting happiness and infinite freedom.

The Editors

PART ONE

The Nature of Devotion

You are Love.
You come from Love.
You are made by Love.
You cannot cease to Love.

Hazrat Inayat Khan

The mind is like the wick of an oil lamp, knowledge is like the flame, but devotion is the oil. Without the fuel of devotion meditation becomes dry, negative and lacking in joy. Therefore, if we wish to truly meditate, we must develop the necessary devotion to support it. But what is true devotion? True devotion is not mere blind worshiping of a God or guru. It is recognizing that the light of awareness in our hearts is also the light of Divine Love. Consciousness itself is caring, compassion, and concern. It nurtures and provides for all beings like a great Mother. Most of our psychological problems arise from a lack of devotion. They exist because we are seeking to be loved rather than willing to give love.

Through the cultivation of devotion or love of God we learn to give love to all beings. We emulate a higher Divine source of love and let it flow through us, not only for our own benefit but for the good of all. A person with devotion cannot ever feel really lonely. Devotion puts us in contact with the Divine presence everywhere, providing a feeling of companionship even with the rocks and the sky. It takes us out of the narrow grooves of the mind and the "separative" compulsions of the ego, placing us beyond ourselves in the greater universe of consciousness. The true devotee sees the Divine beloved everywhere and is at peace with the entire world.

David Frawley
Vedantic Meditation

I

The Nectar of Devotion

by Swami Tejomayananda

Devotion is of the Nature of Love. It is not a mere physical attraction to a person or thing, nor is it an intellectual appreciation of their qualities. The abode of Love is the heart. Thus it is not possible to understand the nature of love through intellectual analysis or logical reasoning alone. Love is a treasure that each of us already has. A wise businessman is one who invests his money wisely and does not waste it. In the same way, we have to invest our capital of love in the Lord. Most of us invest it here, there, and everywhere. However, if we invest it in the Lord, the return will be much greater.

In the *Bhagavad Gītā*, Lord Krishna says that everyone is a devotee of the Lord. Each and every person in this world is seeking joy. That is why people run after money, power, sense pleasures, and so on. But these joys are transient. What people are really seeking is Permanent Bliss and that is only to be found in the Lord. He alone is the source of all bliss. Until we develop total love for Him, and discover this nectar of joy, our search will continue.

Without love, life is meaningless. People who have the love of a beloved, develop a cheerful attitude towards life. Just think how much loftier would be the attitude of someone who enjoys the highest love, the love of the Supreme Lord.

It is said that if spiritual life is a tree, its flowers are self-control and discrimination, the knowledge of right and wrong.

Once these are cultivated, it culminates in the fruit: Knowledge of the Self. Just as a fruit without juice would be tasteless similarly, knowledge without devotion is dry and uninspiring. Thus the nectar of this knowledge is devotion or *bhakti* to the lotus feet of the Lord. Unless this knowledge culminates in devotion, a total Love for the Lord, it is not complete. Devotion is the fulfillment of all spiritual endeavors.

There are two kinds of love in this world, attachment (*āsakti*) and devotion (*bhakti*).

Āsakti is attachment to material objects such as a house, a car, or to people, such as spouse, children, parents, friends, and so on. Attachment, also known as fascination, attraction, or infatuation, is finite and limited to the objects of our desire. Excessive attachment may lead to one's downfall, as one may even perform illegal or immoral actions in order to acquire what is desired.

Bhakti, on the other hand, is devotion to a higher cause for something higher than ourselves. Why do we find it so hard to love others? It is because of our sense of alienation. We consider ourselves to be different from others. It is only when we begin to think of others as ourselves that we rise above our personal limitations. It also makes us see the Lord in all. So *bhakti*, the highest love, is love for the Supreme Lord, and is the means to progress on the path of spirituality.

Some people think of *bhakti* as going to the temple and singing His glories with much emotion. Therefore it may be said that the path of devotion is for emotional people. People who consider themselves to be intellectuals believe that they can only adopt the path of knowledge or *jñāna mārga*. But examples of great saints and sages reveal how they perfectly blended their education and knowledge with a true attitude of Supreme Love for the Lord.

The reason that most of us are unable to love God is that we don't know who or what God is. We can see and touch worldly objects and enjoy them, but where is God? What does He look like? It is difficult to love something or someone whom we do not know. Some people think of God as a judge sitting in heaven, giving out rewards (heaven) and punishments (hell). Many think of Him as a servant who is supposed to do their bidding by granting them whatever they are praying for, and they can forget all about Him the rest of the time. But God is neither servant nor grantor! He is the very Self of all beings. He is That without which nothing could exist. He is like the gold in the ornaments or the clay in the pots. He is the underlying support of the entire creation.

Developing Devotion

There are innumerable ways in which love for the Lord can be expressed. Just like we can express it in different ways to the people that we love. We may want to talk to them, buy them gifts, praise them, want to spend time together, or simply want to just think about them all the time. Similarly, devotees express their love for God in various ways, depending on their aptitude and attitude. Some people think that going to the temple and singing His glories is the way to express devotion. That is one way. There are others who spend hours performing elaborate rituals, chanting numerous prayers or repeating the name of the Lord either at home, or at the temple. Others remember Him at all times in all their activities. Some meditate on the Self in order to realize God within them. While others listen to His glories and attend spiritual discourses. Then there are some who worship Him through work, they act with the attitude that they are doing God's work. This kind of worship is called *karma yoga*. All the ways of worship are good, but the most important ingredient in all is love. Worship without love is just mechanical. It is this attitude of sincere love that turns any activity into devotion for the Lord.

So how does one develop devotion for the Lord? In chapter eleven of the *Bhagavad Gītā*, Lord Krishna says, "Through devotion a person comes to know Me as I am." In reality, if we want to know about anything, be it art, music, or science, we have to develop a love for it. So what we need to do is to develop some sort of relationship with God, what kind does not matter. Some people worship Him as their master (*dāsya bhāva*), a supreme example of this is Hanumanji. Many people look up to God as father or mother. Some think of Lord as their beloved, as did Mirabai, who spent her time singing Lord Krishna's praises. It was also seen in the *gopī* who danced Raas Lila with Him, the bliss that they experienced is indescribable. Still others see God as a child *vātsalya bhāva*, and their attitude is of giving and not wanting anything in return, as did Mother Yashoda with Lord Krishna. Some people love God as a friend, *sākhyā bhāva* as Arjuna did. Lord Krishna says to Arjuna: "You are my devotee and my friend. That is why I am giving you this Knowledge."

The beauty of *bhakti* is that we have the freedom to worship God in whichever form we may choose; be it Rama, Krishna, Shiva, Allah, Jesus, or the formless Infinite Reality. The only requirement is that we must absorb our heart in the Lord. He can then assume whatever form we want Him to have. If our efforts are sincere He will be there for us. He will never fail a loving heart.

The unique feature of the path of devotion (*bhakti mārga*) is that no special qualification is needed to follow it. Any one can develop love. While the path of knowledge (*jñāna yoga*) requires a great intellect and memory, the nature of love is that no special qualities are required. Where there is love, nothing else is required. There is no need to learn elaborate rituals and ceremonies. A devotee is simply asked by the Lord to go to Him with a loving and sincere heart.

Through total devotion to the Lord, the devotee arrives at the cessation of mundane thoughts, and his mind is saturated with thoughts of the Lord at all times. With such a single-pointed mind, his actions are performed with an attitude of service to the Lord, so they are always unselfish. This leads to pu-

7

rity of the mind. Also the devotee feels the Lord's presence in everyone, including himself. This leads to the concept of unity with the Lord and with all beings. Thus in a true devotee we see a culmination of *karma yoga* and *jñāna yoga*.

The language of love is peculiar; words are not needed to express it. Love and service is all that is required. As God's nature is sweetness, in whatever way we partake in it, the result will be sweet. God is compassionate. How much could we benefit if we remember God with love, every day and at every moment! He says, "I am like your servant, waiting for you to call Me."

He became Arjuna's charioteer in the Kurukshetra war upon Arjuna's asking with love and devotion. In the *Śrīmad Bhāgavatam* the Lord says, "My devotee is greater than me." He even changes his own rules for the love of the devotee—like when Lord Krishna broke his own vow of not lifting a weapon in the Mahabharata war to keep Bhishma's words.

Overcoming Obstacles

People often say, "I don't know where to start. I am not good enough to worship the Lord. I am waiting for His blessings." But wise people do not wait. They fill their heart with love for Him, and consider all their activities as worship to Him.

On this path, we may encounter some obstacles, however. For instance, a subtle ego may develop, such as: I am the greatest devotee, or I am the best disciple of my guru. This ego is often very difficult to overcome. The second obstacle is possessiveness, the feeling of my body, my family, and my wealth, and being special. The third is our sense organs, which pull us towards an object of their craving. This pull has tremendous power, and it can delude us very easily. Even great rishis and devotees have been misled.

How do we overcome these obstacles? The best way to overcome them is to be in the company of holy men and holy books (*satsaṅga*). Associate with those whose hearts are ever filled with love for the Lord, and listen to them. As we do so, our attachments slowly diminish, our desires reduce, we develop discrimination and more love flows. There are many examples of people who attained liberation by association with saints, the best one is Dhruva reaching the Lord through his association with Sage Narada.

When encountering obstacles, just remember the name of the Lord with love and devotion. When we feel helpless or powerless we just have to invoke His presence. He is all-powerful and He will certainly help us. Many devotees have overcome tremendous obstacles and hardships by remembering His name. The scriptures say that the name of the Lord is more powerful than the Lord Himself. His name is always with us. It will always protect us.

In the *Śrīmad Bhāgavatam*, we find the child Prahlad teaching his father Hiranyakashyapu the nine ways of devotion:

a) *Śravaṇam*: Listening to his glories. b) *Kīrtanam*: Singing the glories of the Lord. c) *Smaraṇam*: Remembering Him at all times. d) *Pāda-sevanam*: Worshiping Him by serving Him, including service to the people. e) *Arcanam*: Worshiping Him by the performance of rituals and ceremonies. f) *Vandanam*: Bowing before Him, in an attitude of humility. g) *Dāsyam*: Being His servant by carrying on whatever activities He would wish h) *Sākhyam*: Seeing Him as our friend. i) *Ātmanivedanam*: Totally surrendering to Him.

Types of Devotees

There are four kinds of devotees. The *Ārta* is one who experiences sorrow or affliction, and turns to God for help. The *jijñāsu* is one who desires knowledge, and wants to know God. The *arthārthī* is one who wants more money, power, and worldly possessions. And the *jñānī* is one who has no desires, and just wants the Lord Himself.

Love is measured in terms of how much we are willing to sacrifice for the object of our love. Supreme Love is that for which we are ready to sacrifice anything and everything. This raises the question, "What needs to be sacrificed?" It is the ego, our selfishness; the sense of "I" and "mine." The wise person has no ego, no separate identity, he considers himself to be one with the Lord. He sees the Lord within and also in all of creation, therefore he sees the Lord as the very Self of all beings. He loves everyone equally. When he thus loves God, how can he hate anyone? "Love thy neighbor as thyself," is his motto. He is constantly engaged in the welfare of all, and that to Him is service of the Lord. He cannot bear to see anyone suffer, and he considers anyone's pain and suffering like his own. The wise one identifies with the entire creation. He sees himself in all; there is no sense of separateness. He sees the Lord in everyone, serves everyone with devotion, and considers the welfare of others at all times. A person devoted to God in this way gives up selfishness, attachment, and his ego. He has done what needs to be done and has achieved what needs to be achieved.

The nature of a true devotee is that of the *jñānī*. He has achieved *bhakti sudhā*, the nectar of devotion. "Such a devotee is dear to me," says the Lord. We should all aspire for it.

II

Shri Chaitanya: Embodiment of Divine Love

by Swami Pramathananda

The real history of India is the history of the saints and seers, both men and women, which India has produced for the last five thousand years or more. It is they who have guided and molded the destiny of the nation. And it is interesting to note that during the days of national calamity in moral, social, and spiritual fields one such great soul was always born to save the situation.

The advent of Shri Chaitanya took place at a time when India was passing through a great moral, social, and political crisis. He was born in Navadwip in West Bengal in 1485 and lived only for 48 years (1485-1533). The first 24 years of his life were spent as a renowned Sanskrit scholar and the second half of his life was spent as a saint of divine love, teaching and preaching in different parts of India.

The turning point of his life arrived when he came to Gayadham to offer oblations to the departed soul of his father Jagannath Mishra. There he had a vision of God at the temple of Vishnu, and a *Vaishnava* saint, Iswara Puri, initiated him. He went into an ecstatic mood and forgot the outside world entirely. His companions brought him back to Navadwip with great difficulty.

After coming back he could not teach any more in his school. On the other hand, he started to preach to a group of devotees about the divine love of God. Men, women, children, Hindus and Muslims, regardless of caste, creed, color, and religion, joined the group. It was during the period of Muslim rule that through force, temptation, or allurements many Hindus were being converted to Islam. But Shri Chaitanya declared that the devotees of God form a class by themselves. There is no division of high or low among the devotees. This message of oneness brought back the much-needed hope in the minds of the lower class people and they were saved from the danger of leaving their own religion.

In Shri Chaitanya's character we find a wonderful combination of strength and softness. He was as strong as a thunderbolt and as soft as a flower. Once a local Muslim administrator, misguided by others, issued an "Order" to stop Shri Chaitanya from preaching God's name with drums and cymbals, and so on, publicly. The devotees were afraid. But Shri Chaitanya asked all the devotees to assemble at night with all those instruments and lighted firewood in hands. He led a huge procession and marched towards the residence of the Kazi (the administrator). The Kazi was terribly afraid, seeing the great crowd with fire in their hands. He apologized and withdrew the "Order."

But Shri Chaitanya was feeling a divine call in his heart to renounce the world and to become a monk. He took formal vows of *saṁnyāsa* from a great saint, Keshava Bharati.

Now the second half of his life started—preaching the divine love of God. He came to Puri, which is called Jagannath Dham in Orissa. It was an independent kingdom of the Hindus under Pratap Rudra, a powerful king. The king, his court Pandit Sarva Bhauma and his Governor of the South, Roy Ramananda, all became Shri Chaitanya's followers.

In every religion we find two basic principles—the ideal to be realized and the method of realization. All the prophets and scriptures proclaim the truth that God exists and the goal of human life is to realize God or in other words to know the Supreme Truth.

Broadly speaking, there are four ways to realize God—the

way of devotion, the way of knowledge, the way of meditation and the way of karma. The way of devotion, which appeals to the majority of mankind, requires that we focus our attention away from worldly matters and direct it to the spiritual plane. This, in essence, was the message of divine love that Shri Chaitanya demonstrated in his life and teachings.

Love, as a force of attraction, operates at different levels, namely, material, human, and spiritual. At the material level, one is attracted to worldly possessions, such as wealth, health, name and fame. At the human level, love joins friend with friend, parents with children, husband with wife, and so on. There is also, of course, the love of music and poetry, which is more impersonal and enduring than human love.

But spiritual love is, by far, the most profound. At the spiritual level, love unites man with God. When love of God fills the heart, all other forms of love pale into insignificance. As Shri Ramakrishna said, "As the bigger star rises, the smaller ones become dim. Then when the moon rises, the biggest star becomes pale, and finally when the sun rises, the moon and all the other stars are engulfed in its light. God is like the sun, and those who love God are not interested in worldly love, physical or intellectual."

Distinct Features of Divine Love

Shri Chaitanya distinguished divine love from other kinds of love with respect to three characteristics. First, divine love knows no bargaining; rather it is based on sacrifice, not expecting anything in return. Second, where divine love exists, there is no fear (and conversely, where fear exists, there can be no divine love). Third, there is no jealousy or hatred. A slave, for example, cannot love his master. Love is both the means and the end.

In human relationships, on the other hand, love often functions more like shop keeping. The love we give others is little, though what we expect in return is much. Divine love, in contrast, functions wholly differently—it knows no bargaining and carries no expectations. The *gopī*, the milkmaids of Vrindavan, loved Lord Krishna in this fashion. This calls to mind a story: The great sage Narada once found Lord Krishna suffering from a headache. When Narada, who was capable of moving through the three worlds, asked what he could do to help the Lord, he was told that the headache could be cured only if dust from under a devotee's feet was put on his forehead. Narada was shocked, for it was well known that if the dust from under a devotee's feet were put on the Lord's forehead, that devotee would be eternally doomed. It would surely be impossible to find such a person. In spite of the immense difficulty of the task, sage Narada traveled over the three worlds to find such a devotee. Finally he came to Vrindavan, the sacred forest by the river Yamuna near Mathura, the birthplace of Krishna, where he played with the *gopī*, and especially with Radha. When the *gopī* heard that their beloved Lord was suffering and were told about the remedy, they did not hesitate to give the dust from their own feet. Narada wondered if they knew of the consequences. They did; but their sole concern, they said, was for their Lord, no matter what they suffered as a result!

In the *Rāmāyaṇa*, there is a touching incident when Rama and Lakshmana went to a pond to drink water. They planted their bows in the ground and after refreshing themselves, came to retrieve the bows. Rama was shocked to find that his bow had blood on it. Looking at the ground, he discovered a frog, which had been pierced with the bow. Rama asked, "Why did you not croak or make some noise so that I would know you were there?" The frog replied, "When I am attacked by anyone, I call out your name. But when Ramachandra himself has pierced my body, I accept it as his grace." That is the attitude of the devotee. Whatever comes is God's grace. It is complete surrender.

The *gopī's* love for Lord Krishna thus exemplifies the nature of divine love. The same notion of love without expectation is found in other religions—for example, in the lines uttered by Saint Francis of Assisi, the 16th century Christian saint:

Lord make me an instrument of thy peace;
Where there is hatred, let me sow love;
Where there is injury, pardon;
Where there is doubt, faith;
Where there is despair, hope;
Where there is darkness, light;
Where there is sadness, joy.

A similar devotion was expressed by Rabbia, an eighth-century Muslim saint, who said, "My love for Allah leaves no room inside me to hate anybody, not even Satan. I see the face of Allah in everything and everywhere." Her love for the divine knew no fear, nor any hatred—the divine manifested itself in everything she saw. This was also the case with St. Theresa of Avila, another 16th century Christian saint (and incidentally, a contemporary of Mira Bai, the princess who renounced the world out of her great love for Krishna). St. Theresa taught that through divine love, all obstacles could be overcome, since all is a manifestation of divine love.

There are two stages in the practice of *bhakti yoga*: the preliminary (*gaunī*) and the higher (*parā-bhakti*). The preliminary is problematic because it may lead to fanaticism. Fanatics practice their own faith to perfection but are intolerant of other faiths. However, fanaticism can be overcome at the higher stage of divine love, for here one discovers that all faiths lead to the same Godhead. Shri Ramakrishna tells us that the capacity for divine love can be engendered through *japam* (repetition of the name of the Lord), by keeping holy company, and by reading sacred texts and making pilgrimages to holy places, among other spiritual practices.

Expressions of Divine Love

Lastly, there are five different ways of expressing divine love—*śānta* (harmonious peace or stillness); *dāsya* (in which God is the master and devotee the servant) as Hanuman for instance was the servant of Ramachandra; *sākhya* (deep friendship, that

15

which existed between Krishna and his cowherd friends, or between Krishna and Arjuna); *vātsalya* (the tender love of parents for their child as Yasoda's love for Krishna); and *mādhurya* (the attitude of a wife or beloved towards her husband or lover as demonstrated by Radha and Krishna in the *Bhāgavata-Purāṇa*). This most intense aspect of divine love is, however, not easy to understand; nor is it possible for impure souls.

Swami Vivekananda describes it thus: "Ah, that most marvelous passage of his [Krishna's] life, the most difficult to understand, and which none ought to attempt to understand until he has become perfectly chaste and pure, that most marvelous expansion of love, allegorized and expressed in that beautiful play at Vrindavan, which none can understand but he who has become mad with love, drunk deep of the cup of love! Who can understand the throes of the love of the *gopī*—the very ideal of love, love that wants nothing, love that even does not care for heaven, love that does not care for anything in this world or the world to come?... They [the *Gopī*] hated every adjective that was applied to Krishna; they did not care to know that he was almighty.... The only thing they understood was that he was infinite love, that was all."

The *Yugala Mūrti* or conjugal images of Shri Krishna and Shri Radha are representative of the divine. They are a representation of the entwinement of the spirit (*puruṣa*) and matter (*prakṛti*). In other words, the Radha-Krishna idol is the same as the Shiva-Shakti idol. One cannot exist without the other, just as fire cannot exist without its power to burn.

Shri Chaitanya made a pilgrimage to Varanasi, Prayag (Allahabad) and Vrindavan preaching *bhakti yoga*—the love aspect of God. He sent his very faithful disciples Rupa and Sanatan to Vrindavan who were very close ministers of the Nawab of Bengal before joining the group of Shri Chaitanya. They discovered and restored all those places associated with Shri Krishna by practicing great *tapasyā*. Those temples and buildings had been destroyed by Muslim rulers and the places were covered by jungles at that time.

To establish an ideal householder's life he convinced Nityananda (Avadhut), his very close companion, to marry and live as an ideal householder in Navadwip. And Nityananda obeyed.

May the love he preached manifest in us, and make us pure in thought, word, and deed!

III

Divine Love

by Hazrat Inayat Khan

Love is directed by the intelligence; therefore each person chooses his object of love according to his evolution. That appears to him most deserving of love, which is in accordance with the grade of his evolution. There is a saying in the East. "As the soul is, so are its angels." The donkey would prefer thistles to roses.

The consciousness that is awakened to the material world has its object of love only in earthly beauties. The consciousness active through the mind finds its object in thought and among the thoughtful. The consciousness awakened through the heart loves love and the loving ones. And the consciousness awakened in the soul loves the spirit and the spiritual.

Silent love, which is the divine essence in man, becomes active, living, on seeing the vision of beauty. Beauty may be explained as perfection, perfection in every aspect of beauty. Not love alone is God or the essence of God, but beauty also, even in its limited aspects, shows itself as glimpses of the perfect Being. The mineral kingdom develops into gold, silver, diamonds, rubies, and emeralds, showing perfection in it; the fruit and flower, their sweetness and fragrance, show perfection in the vegetable kingdom; form, figure, and youth show perfection in the animal kingdom; and it is the beauty of personality which is significant of perfection in the human being.

There are some people in this world whose life is absorbed in the pursuit of gold and silver, gems and jewels; they would sacrifice anything or anybody to acquire the object of their love.

There are others whose life is engaged in the beautiful vision of fruits, flowers, flowerbeds, and gardens; perhaps they have no other interest besides. There are some who are absorbed in the admiration of the youth and beauty of the opposite sex, and nothing else seems to them worth more. There are others who are won by the beauty of someone's personality, and have entirely devoted themselves to the one they love, both their here and their hereafter.

Everyone has his object of love according to his standard of beauty, and at the same time each one loves the perfection of the Divine Being in a certain aspect. When the seer sees this, no one, wise or foolish, sinner or virtuous, remains blameworthy in his sight. He sees in every heart the needle of the compass that turns to one and the same Being. "God is beautiful and He loves beauty," as it is said in the Hadith.

Preparing for Divine Love

Man is never capable of loving God in heaven when his sympathy has not even been awakened to the beauty of the earth.

A village maiden was on her way to see her beloved. She passed by a Mullah who was saying prayers. In her ignorance she walked in front of him, which is forbidden by the religious law. The Mullah was very angry, and when she, returning, again passed near him, he scolded her for her mistake. He said, "How sinful, O girl, on your part to cross in front of me while I was offering my prayer." She said, "What does prayer mean?" He said, "I was thinking of God, the Lord of the heavens and of the earth." She said, "I am sorry. I don't know yet of God and His prayers, but I was on my way to my beloved, and, thinking of my beloved, I did not see you praying. I wonder how you, who were in the thought of God, could see me?" Her words so much impressed the Mullah that he said to her, "From this moment, O maiden, you are my teacher. It is I who should learn from you."

Someone once came to Jami and asked to be his *mureed.*

Jami said, "Have you ever loved anyone in life?" He said, "No." Jami said, "Then go, and love someone, and then come to me."

It is for this reason that great teachers and masters have often had difficulty in awakening the love of God in the average man. Parents give their child a doll so that the child may know how to dress it, how to be kind to it, how to look after it, how to love and admire it, which trains the child to become a loving mother in the future. Without this training the later course would be difficult. Divine love would be as strange to the average person as the cares of motherhood to a girl who has not yet played enough with dolls.

A *mureed* had been a long time in the service of a spiritual guide, but he could make no progress and was not inspired. He went to the teacher and said, "I have seen very many *mureeds* being inspired, but it is my misfortune that I cannot advance at all, and now I must give up hope and leave you." The teacher advised him to spend the last days of his stay in a house near the Khankah, and every day he sent him very good food and told him to cease the spiritual practices and to lead a comfortable and restful life. On the last day he sent the *mureed* a basket of fruit by a fair damsel. She set the tray down and immediately went away, though he wished to detain her. Her beauty and charm were so great, and he was now so much disposed to admire and was so much won by them, that he could think of nothing else. Every hour and every minute he longed only to see her again. His longing increased every moment. He forgot to eat, he was full of tears and sighs, finding his heart now warmed and melted by the fire of love. After some time, when the teacher visited the disciple, with one glance he inspired him. "Even steel can be molded if it be heated in the fire," and so it is with the heart which is melted by the fire of love.

It is love's wine, which is called *Sherab-i-Kouthar*, the wine found in the heavens. When the intoxication of love increases in man, people call him blindly in love or madly in love, because people wide-awake to the illusion of the surface consider themselves to be the only ones wide-awake; but their wakefulness is to the delusion, not to reality. Although the lover is called crazy, his craze for one object of the world of illusion makes him gradually free from all delusion around him. If he succeeds in attaining to this he enjoys his union with the beloved in his happy vision. Then no time is needed to lift from his sight the veil of the one object which he loved; as is said in the Koran, "We will lift the veil from thine eyes and thy sight will be keen."

It is natural for a lover to become infatuated with someone whom he admires, with whom he desires union; but no one object in the world is so perfect as fully to satisfy the aspiration of the loving heart. This is the stumbling block that causes every beginner in love to fall. The successful travelers on the path of love are those whose love is so beautiful that it provides all the beauty that their ideal lacks. The lover by doing this in time rises above the changeable and limited beauty of the beloved, but begins to see into the beloved's inner being; in other words, the exterior of the beloved was only a means of drawing the love out of the heart of the lover, but the love led him from the external to the innermost being of the ideal of his love. When in the ideal the lover has realized the unlimited and perfect Being, whether he loves man or God, he is in fact, in either case a blissful lover.

In this the journey through the path of idealism is ended and a journey through the divine ideal is begun, for the God-ideal is necessary for the attainment of life's perfection. Man then seeks for a perfect object of love, idealizing God, the whole Being, the Infinite, who is above all the world's lights and shades, good and ill, who is pure from all limitations, births or deaths, unchangeable, inseparable from us, all-pervading, present always before the vision of his lover.

Crushing the Ego

When love is true it takes away selfishness, for this is the only solution to wipe off the ego. The English phrase "to fall in love" conveys the idea of the true nature of love. It is a fall indeed from

21

the pedestal of the ego to the ground of nothingness, but at the same time it is this fall, which leads to a rise, for as low as the lover falls so high he rises in the end. The lover falls in love as a seed is thrown in the ground. Both appear to be destroyed, but both in time spring up and flourish and bear fruit for the ever-hungry world.

Man's greatest enemy in the world is his ego, the thought of self. This is the germ from which springs all evil in man. Even the virtues of the egoist turn into sin, and his small sins into great crimes. All religions and philosophies teach man to crush it, and there is nothing that can crush it better than love. The growth of love is the decay of the ego. Love in its perfection entirely frees the lover from all selfishness, for love may be called in other words annihilation. "Whoever enters the school of lovers, the first lesson he learns is not to be."

Unity is impossible without love, for it is love only, which can unite. Each expression of love signifies the attainment of union as its object, and two things cannot unite unless one of them becomes nothing. No one knows this secret of life except the lover. Iraqi says in his verse, "When I, without having loved, went to Ka'ba and knocked at the gate, a voice came: 'What didst thou accomplish in thy home that thou hast come forth?' And when I went, having lost myself in love, and knocked at the gate of Ka'ba, a voice said: 'Come, Come, O Iraqi, thou art ours.'"

If there is anything that works against the vanity of the ego, it is love. The nature of love is to surrender; there is no one in the world who does not surrender. The world of variety, which has divided life into limited parts, naturally causes every lesser one to surrender to the greater. And, again, for every greater one there is another still greater in relation to whom he is smaller, and for every smaller one there is another still smaller, in relation to whom he is greater. And as every soul is by its nature compelled to surrender to perfection in all its grades, the only thing that matters is whether it be a willing surrender or an unwilling surrender. The former comes by love, the latter is made through helplessness, which makes life wretched. It moves the Sufi when he reads in the Koran that the perfect Being asked the imperfect souls, the children of Adam, "Who is thy Lord?" They, conscious of their imperfections, said humbly, "Thou art our Lord." Surrender is a curse when, with coldness and help-lessness, one is forced to surrender; but the same becomes the greatest joy when it is made with love and all willingness.

Love is the practice of the moral of Suluk, the way of benefi-cence. The lover's pleasure is in the pleasure of the beloved. The lover is satisfied when the beloved is fed. The lover is vain when the beloved is adorned. "Who in life blesses the one who curses him? Who in life admires the one who hates him? Who in life proves faithful to the one who is faithless? No other than a lover." And in the end the lover's self is lost from his vision and only the beloved's image, the desired vision, is before him for-ever.

Love is the essence of all religion, mysticism, and philoso-phy, and the one who has learnt this love fulfils the purpose of religion, ethics, and philosophy, and the lover is raised above all diversities of faiths and beliefs.

IV

Love for God

by Swami Ashokananda

This morning we are concerned with the path of devotion, or of love, in which one approaches the object of search with the heart. Love belongs to the heart. We may have an *idea* of love, which might belong to the intellect or to reason, but actual love is a part of our heart. And since most of us seem to be full of heart, or I should say, since most of us approach things with a craving of our heart, with the hope that we shall find some pleasure or happiness or fulfillment out of it, when we turn to spiritual life, we find ourselves most fitted and most inclined to follow the path of emotion. And since emotion seems to be the closest thing to most of us, it does not require any kind of explanation; it is already clear to us. Although the object of our emotion or love could be anything—it could be money, it could be name and fame—but more often than not, it is another person, another living being; so this part of the path of devotion is also very clear to us. To put it simply, this path is an effort on our part to love God instead of loving our father and mother, or husband, wife, children, or things such as name and fame, or wealth and possessions, and so on. Our heart delights in these things in this life, which we generally call worldly life, because it is not enlightened. But when the same love is concentrated upon a spiritual object, such as God, then it can be called *bhakti* or devotion.

Now, there is no use saying that we do not have a great deal of love in our heart. If you have any doubt about it, just see with what tremendous tenacity we cling to a thing. We cling to ourselves, to our own comforts, to our own life. We cling to our near and dear ones or to our possessions, and we would do anything to hold on to them. Such love is manifest not only in human beings, but also in subhuman creatures. It seems to be the most noticeable thing in every living being. So our problem is not how to cultivate love but how to direct this same wealth of love, this same powerful love towards God instead of towards the objects to which it has been going. A process is called for, and I would like to talk about that process or the method by which this redirection of our love can take place.

Since, as I have already pointed out, the path of devotion has been most abundantly sought after, it would follow that a great deal of information about it has been available. Almost every religion has taught it. Even Buddhism, which did not begin with love for God, very soon became transformed into a path of devotion. The Buddhists simply replaced God by Lord Buddha himself. They began to install his image, to sing his glory, to meditate upon him; they did all the things any devotee would do. So in almost every religion you find the path of devotion, and therefore, a good deal of information as to how to practice it. Although this path does not differ very much in the various religions, I shall present to you those methods spoken of by Hindu teachers.

Now, like all other paths, the path of devotion presupposes that we have undergone the necessary transformation called self-discipline. It is no use talking of religion to people who are immersed in the world. They may talk about God, they may hear about God, and they may occasionally discuss God with you, but their heart is wholly in worldly things, in sense objects. Not that we are condemning them. Hinduism never does that, because it believes in reincarnation and thinks that in every life the soul through its own experiences undergoes change and eventually will realize a spiritually desirable state; all that we say about worldly people, is that their time has not yet come.

That's a very favorite expression. Say for some reason a worldly man becomes interested in spiritual practice and goes to

SWAMI ASHOKANANDA

a Hindu teacher. The teacher will look at him and talk with him,
and if he has insight, he will say, "The time is not yet. Go back
to the world, live the worldly life in the best way." You see, even
in worldly life there is a method; there are different ways of being worldly. In one way you will go deeper and deeper into
bondage. In another way you will gradually become liberated.

It is generally said that those who live in the world performing their duties relative to their position in life—pleasure is not
their only motive but also duty, at least both are equally present—
gradually overcome sense desires. Most religions have spoken
about this. In India we have divided religious teachings into two
parts and have left the part of restrained worldly living to the Brah-
min priests. They are worldly teachers, they are married and
have children, but they are good people, and they have acquainted
themselves with the scriptures. They themselves are trying to
practice this way of living, and so they can tell others, they can
say, "Brother, live like this. If you go too much into the world,
you will get burnt up by worldly desires. Live in a restrained
way." There is a way by which worldliness can be gradually
changed into a real desire for spiritual knowledge but until that
desire has come, you cannot practice religion seriously, no matter what path you might follow.

How are you to know that this condition has come to you?
You know it by the state of your own mind. You will find that
from time to time your mind moves away from all the things of
the world. It wants to become quiet, as if in that quietness it will
find something; and from time to time the mind does acquire an
inner quietness. Just as on a stormy day when the wind is blus-
tery, from time to time there are quiet moments, in the same
way, the stormy mind, as it were, reaches those points of quietness. When that condition has come and you try to increase that
quietness of mind, you cultivate religion. As a matter of fact,
you feel a desire to think about God or to find a person who talks
about God. Then you can gradually rise to a better condition of
the mind, and you can practice religion much more seriously. In
the path of devotion there has to be a desire to know God, to love

Him. The heart craves to know Him; the heart likes to think about Him. Maybe again, after an hour or so, the mind goes back to material things; nevertheless for one hour the mind has dwelt on God: it *wants* to dwell on God.

It is said that when a person has reached that stage and starts the practice of devotion, his progress can be divided into two parts. One is called formal devotion, and the other, the higher part, is called the path of pure love. In other words, after you have followed formal devotion, you reach a state when spontaneous love of God has become very strong in your heart and becomes the motive force; your practices follow from this spontaneous love that has filled your heart.

Obstacles to Spiritual Growth

In the first part of devotion, which is called formal devotion, *vaidhī bhakti*, there are certain prescriptions, *vidhi*, and also certain prohibitions, *niṣedha*. To speak of the prohibitions first, you should give up all those things that are apt to take your heart away from God. If you are still in the world and have not become so overwhelmed by love for God that you are free from worldly responsibilities, then you perform those duties as an offering to the Lord, but you do no more than is necessary. Further, if say you are working in an office, you could do your work and you could also indulge in lots of gossip with your fellow workers. But that latter part you will find you cannot do; you may not indulge in gossip.

It is not only as an example that I am mentioning this, it is also an important prohibition. All teachers of devotion have said that indulging in gossip is one of the greatest obstacles to spiritual progress. As a matter of fact, it is an obstacle along any path, but teachers of devotion have particularly emphasized it. What then are you to do? You are to talk with your friends about God. Of course I understand that in America to talk about God is somewhat indecent; you must not do it openly. Well, there is a good side to that. If something is close to your heart, you do not want to speak about it; you rarely give expression to something very deep in you. On the other hand, if you do not speak about God, even with devotees, then what will you speak about?

You *should* speak about God with fellow devotees, but you have to be sure that they are devotees. At first, you might get acquainted with a person on the basis of spiritual contact. Afterwards, unless you are very cautious, the friendship will turn to just a worldly association. At the very first opportunity a woman, if she is married, wants to speak about her husband or about her children. Well, men also have their wives and children. They don't speak of them so much, but a man will carry a picture of his baby in his wallet and show it to everyone. That is the nature of both men and women. But since you are a devotee, you are neither man nor woman; you are a child of God, and your behavior should be different. You must not indulge in those things unless it is necessary. You should consciously make a point of speaking about God alone, and expect that others would speak of God with you. Thereby you can avoid lots of gossip.

In other words, anything that takes your heart away from God and makes you forget Him you should avoid. Doing unnecessary things, going to unnecessary places, remaining lazy without doing anything—all these things are to be avoided, because they are all obstacles to spiritual growth, particularly to the growth of devotion in one's own heart.

Practices for Developing Devotion

As regards *vidhi*, that which we should do, many practices have been prescribed. One practice is to continually exercise self-examination. "Self-examination" does not mean any kind of psychological analysis, but, rather, an examination of the mind with a very definite purpose. For instance, after the day is over, you pass the whole day in review and see whether everything was done right. By "doing right" two things are meant. One is that you have done your duty in the right spirit and in the right way. Another, much more important, meaning is that you did those things in a spirit of detachment—which is called *karma yoga*—and that you remembered God as much as you could, that you were alert and did not allow time to be wasted or let yourself become too much involved in your work. That kind of self-examination is very desirable. Of course, it goes without saying that on such examination we shall always find that we have fallen far short of our expectations. So we should determine that the next day we shall avoid wasting time or doing things in the wrong spirit or in the wrong way.

Another kind of self-examination is philosophical and can be undertaken whenever one has a little time. It is to ask oneself, "Who am I? What am I? Where have I come from? What am I doing here? Where am I going? What is the goal of my life?" And so on and so forth.

At first these questions might appear to be artificial efforts on your part, but *all* spiritual living—as a matter of fact, all self-improvement—consists in consciously and deliberately practicing those things which will be natural to us only when we have reached a higher stage of our growth. Self-improvement does not mean that we behave spontaneously according to our present nature or instincts. If we were to do that, then we could not make any progress, and believe me, many of us would appear much worse than we are. But while we know that we have a lower side (and a stronger side it maybe), we also are aware of a higher side, and we try to live up to that. There is artificiality about it, but that does not mean that it is not sincere. In spiritual life also, we do that. It may not be natural for you to ask these questions, "Who am I?" and so on. But you *should* ask them of yourself, and you should try to find clear answers to them because when you have reached a higher state of spiritual growth, these questions will come spontaneously to you. You are only anticipating what is going to happen, and by such anticipation you are pushing yourself forward. So that kind of philosophical self-examination is very necessary.

Another thing that is prescribed is this: in everything we

should try to cultivate non-egotism. Since at present we do not know what our self is, we should not give importance to our ego. In our unenlightened state we think our ego *is* our self, which, of course, is not true, and since we have not found the answer to what our self really is, we should at least try to abolish this ego—this false self. When we work without attachment, disinterestedly, we are dealing a blow to the ego. At the same time we should try to see greatness in all others. If we do not see greatness anywhere, neither within ourselves nor in others, then there is danger to us, because the food of our soul, or of our mind and heart, is greatness. If we do not recognize greatness in others in one form or another, our inner life will become blasted; it will dry up.

Of course, thinking of God is thinking of greatness, but since we cannot think of God, let us surround ourselves by the greatness in others, particularly in the people with whom we are in constant contact. Yes, in everyone there is greatness, and if you cannot see any greatness in their mind or in their behavior, you can at least remind yourself that God dwells in the heart of every being. At least that much we can do. But if we are intent upon it, we can really discover true greatness in almost everyone. … All of these practices are very desirable.

V

Tommy

by Father John Powell

About fifteen years ago, I stood watching my university students file into the classroom for our first session in the Theology of Faith. That was the day I first saw Tommy. My eyes and my mind both blinked. He was combing his long flaxen hair, which hung six inches below his shoulders. It was the first time I had ever seen a boy with hair that long. I guess it was just coming into fashion then. I know in my mind that it isn't what's on your head but in it that counts, but on that day I was unprepared and my emotions flipped. I immediately filed Tommy under "S" for strange. ... Very strange.

Tommy turned out to be the "atheist in residence" in my Theology of Faith course. He constantly objected to, smirked at, or whined about the possibility of an unconditionally loving Father-God. We lived with each other in relative peace for one semester, although I admit he was for me at times a serious pain in the back pew. When he came up at the end of the course to turn in his final exam, he asked in a slightly cynical tone: "Do you think I'll ever find God?" I decided instantly on a little shock therapy. "No!" I said very emphatically. "Oh," he responded, "I thought that was the product you were pushing." I let him get five steps from the classroom door and then called out: "Tommy, I don't think you'll ever find Him, but I am absolutely certain that He will find you!" He shrugged a little and left my class and my life (temporarily). I felt slightly disappointed at the thought that he had missed my clever line: "He will find you!" At least I thought it was clever.

Later I heard that Tom was graduated and I was duly grateful. Then a sad report. I heard that Tommy had terminal cancer. Before I could search him out, he came to see me. His body was badly wasted, and the long hair had all fallen out as a result of chemotherapy. But his eyes were bright and his voice was firm, for the first time, I think.

"Tommy, I've thought about you so often. I hear you are sick!" I blurted out.

"Oh yes, very sick. I have cancer in both lungs. It's a matter of weeks."

"Can you talk about it, Tom?"

"Sure, what would you like to know?"

"What's it like to be only twenty-four and dying?"

"Well, it could be worse."

"Like what?"

"Well, like being fifty and having no values or ideals, like being fifty and thinking that booze, seducing women, and making money are the real biggies in life."

I began to look through my mental file cabinet under "S" where I had filed Tom as strange. (I swear that everybody I try to reject by classification of odd is send back into my life to educate me.)

Opening to Love

"But what I really came to you about," Tom said, "is something you said to me on the last day of class." (He remembered)

He continued, "I asked you if you thought I would ever find God and you said, 'No!' which surprised me. Then you said, 'But He will find you.' I thought about that a lot, even though my search for God was hardly intense at that time. (My clever line. He thought about that a lot!)

"But when the doctors removed a lump from my groin and told me that it was malignant, then I got serious about locating

God. And when the malignancy spread into my vital organs, I really began banging bloody fists against the bronze doors of heaven. But God did not come out. In fact, nothing happened. Did you ever try anything for a long time with great effort and with no success? You get psychologically glutted, fed up with trying. And then you quit. Well, one day I woke up, and instead of throwing a few more futile appeals over that high brick wall to a God who may be or may not be there, I just quit. I decided that I didn't really care... about God, about an afterlife, or anything like that.

"I decided to spend what time I had left doing something more profitable. I thought about you and your class and I remembered something else you had said: 'The essential sadness is to go through life without loving. But it would be almost equally sad to go through life and leave this world without ever telling those you loved that you had loved them.'

"So I began with the hardest one: my dad. He was reading a newspaper when I approached him.

'Dad.'

'Yes, what?' He asked without lowering the newspaper.

'Dad, I would like to talk with you.'

'Well, talk.'

'I mean it's really important.'

The newspaper came down three slow inches, 'What is it?'

'Dad, I love you. I just wanted you to know that.'"

Tom smiled at me and said with obvious satisfaction, as though he felt a warm and secret joy flowing inside of him. "The newspaper fluttered to the floor. Then my father did two things I could never remember him ever doing before. He cried and he hugged me. And we talked all night, even though he had to go to work the next morning. It felt so good to be close to my father, to see his tears, to feel his hug, to hear him say that he loved me.

"It was easier with my mother and little brother. They cried with me, too, and we hugged each other, and started saying real nice things to each other. We shared the things we had been keeping secret for so many years. I was only sorry about one thing: that I had waited so long. Here I was, in the shadow of death, and I was just beginning to open up to all the people I had actually been close to.

"Then, one day I turned around and God was there. He didn't come to me when I pleaded with Him. I guess I was like an animal trainer holding out a hoop, 'C'mon, jump through. 'C'mon, I'll give you three days, three weeks.' Apparently God does things in His own way and at His own hour.

"But the important thing is that He was there. He found me. You were right. He found me even after I stopped looking for Him."

"Tommy," I practically gasped, "I think you are saying something very important and much more universal than you realize. To me, at least, you are saying that the surest way to find God is not to make Him a private possession, a problem solver, or an instant consolation in time of need, but rather by opening to love. You know, Saint John said that as well. He said 'God is love, and anyone who lives in love is living with God and God is living in Him.'

"Tom, could I ask you a favor? You know, when I had you in class you were a real pain. But (laughingly) you can make it all up to me now. Would you come into my present Theology of Faith course and tell them what you have just told me? If I told them the same thing, it wouldn't be half as effective as if you were to tell them."

"Ooh, I was ready for you, but I don't know if I'm ready for your class."

"Tom, think about it. If and when you are ready, give me a call."

In a few days Tommy called, said he was ready for the class, that he wanted to do that for God and for me. So we scheduled a date. However, he never made it. He had another appointment, far more important then the one with my class and me. Of course, his life was not really ended by his death, only changed. He made the great step from faith into vision. He found a life far more beautiful than the human eye has ever seen or the human ear has ever heard or the human mind has ever imagined.

Before he died, we talked one last time. "I'm not going to make it to your class," he said.

"I know Tom."

"Will you tell them for me? Will you tell the whole world for me?"

"I will, Tom. I'll tell them. I'll do my best."

So, to all of you who have been kind enough to hear this simple statement about love, thank you for listening. And to you Tom, somewhere in the sunlit, verdant hills of heaven, I told them, Tommy, as best I could.

PART TWO

The Way of Love

Love is not love,
if it does not serve and sacrifice.

Swami Chinmayananda

The Sanskrit term *śraddhā* has a more comprehensive meaning than the English word faith; it means a sense of trust in one's higher Self, in that which is more than body and which sustains the body. Until this deeper faith is awakened in a person, he will take the attitude of being the doer and will depend upon his own human powers, which will always fail him. True discrimination alone can show the way to true self-reliance, and it alone gives us true faith. Do not imagine that anyone can have true faith in God who has no faith in himself. The coward and weakling never has faith in God. He may pretend that he has, but he invariably falls when he meets with difficulties. It is only the spiritually strong man who can have real faith in God and faith in himself as part of God.

Swami Paramananda
Faith is Power

The more one allows the feeling of gratitude to spread in one's being, to express itself in spirit and in act, the more one is lifted up in consciousness, the more one is purified. Gratitude is a quality that purifies and expands the consciousness. It strikes at the root of ego and selfishness and makes room for true humility, facilitates the enlargement of the being by relating it to a wider and still wider circle of the Manifestation. Thus gratitude is a positive help in the growth of the spiritual consciousness. Again, gratitude, the capacity for gratitude grows with progress in spiritual life. For the deeper, higher or inner the ranges of the consciousness attained, the more spontaneously and abundantly wells gratitude in streams of self-giving and love.

The Mother

Spiritual Communion

VI

Questions and Answers

with Swami Chinmayananda

Q: What is Devotion?

A: Devotion is defined in various ways by various teachers, but the one thing that is common in all of them is the element of love. A mind totally turned towards God in love, demanding nothing—not even liberation—is a mind filled with devotion. A constant flow of thoughts in love toward the Supreme is devotion. Longing for no one else, nothing else but the Lord, this attitude of the heart is love. This state is called exclusive love (*ananya prema*) and this total love for the Lord is devotion according to sage Narada, the author of *Nārada Bhakti Sūtra*.

Q: Does divine grace act when we reach the limit of the finite and try to attain the Infinite?

A: The Lord, the Divine, and His grace are not two separate things; they are one and the same. The sun and sunlight can never be two different things; sunlight is the very nature of the sun. Sweetness is the nature of sugar. Heat is the nature of fire. The Lord *is* divine grace.

Therefore, God cannot give grace until you allow Him to enter your life. To invoke Him is to invite His grace. To the extent the heart is open for the inflow of the Higher, to that extent we are under the influence of the grace of the Lord. When we try to reach the outer limits of the finite and enter the realm of the Infinite, it is God's grace alone that functions in those dark and dreary moments before the cheerful dawn.

Q: What is the highest Moral Truth?

A: Love is the greatest morality given to man and hence "Love Thyself" is the greatest moral injunction which all scriptures and Vedas tirelessly repeat. Unless the student is prepared to receive this great advice, however, he is apt to misunderstand the great Vedic injunction as an advice to love the body and to cater to all low thoughts and ideas. "Love thyself" does not mean loving the body or meekly obeying the mind and the intellect. The body, mind, and intellect are a gross matter-envelopment, that have come to seemingly limit the illimitable Supreme Consciousness, which is the real Self in us all. By identifying with our false matter-envelopment, we have projected ourselves into the world as a separate ego, and all our doubts on morality and spirituality have come to confuse us.

The shifting of our identification to the real Self is to live automatically the highest moral and spiritual life. This is accomplished *through* love, *in* love, *as* love. Love alone is the law and the life of the Self. Self-Realization is the experience of love in its absolute nature. "Realize thyself." You have loved yourself the most. And thereafter you know nothing but love for the outside world. There is no greater moral truth than Love. LOVE. L-O-V-E.

When the devotee's mind melts at the contemplation of the loving form and the infinite qualities of the Lord, in the warmth of his supreme single-pointed love, the sublime fusion of finite with the Infinite takes place. At that supreme moment of bliss in the dynamic experience of the whole, there is no individualistic part beyond the whole that could converse with it. At the time of God-consciousness, that is, during the vision of the Lord, in the infinite embrace of the Reality, the unreal totally fades away. It is ignorance that had given the devotee, till this culminating point in spiritual practices, the false notion that he is merely a part of the whole and that he is the seeker. With *Īśvara Darśana* comes the real Knowledge that God alone IS... that the I-conception was false. The devotee in a flash of illumination realizes that it was only the Lord of his heart within him that played the great Divine Play of seeing, hearing, smelling, tasting, and touching the world of objects which in themselves are also nothing but the Lord's own manifestations. When the ego dies away what remains is nothing but an Infinite homogeneous Bliss experience which is GOD.

Where there is God, there the I-sense cannot be: where the I-sense is, there God is indeed far away!

Q: How can an aspirant attain transparent sincerity and earnestness in the quest for God?

A: Sincerity and earnestness are the flowers of the Love Plant that grows in the garden of the heart. In cultivating these flowers the gardener has to prepare the soil, sow the seed, water the plant, and protect the crop. Then it will blossom forth in the thrills of the springtime.

The imperfection in the world of objects provides us with sorrows and despairs of life, which plough the field of the heart. *Japa*, the repetition of the Lord's names, is the sowing of the right seed. With regular and intense meditation upon the form of the Lord of his Heart the seeker waters the seedlings. Truthfulness (*satyam*), non-injury (*ahimsā*) and celibacy (*brahmacarya*) constitute three posts around the plant. Truthfulness is at the intellectual level, non-injury is at the mental level, and celibacy is at the physical level. Living up to these principles constitutes the right conduct of life. Along with these principles, the help of *dharma* (the rules of moral and ethical living) a fence should be put up to guard it from the ravages of grazing animals! In time the plant grows, and in its own maturity, in the springtime (as the heart gains in the Lord's grace) it blooms forth into the noble flowers of sweet-scented sincerity and earnestness. The buzzing bee of *mumukṣuttva* (an all-consuming eagerness to break the chains of limitations and reach the freedom of the beyond) would then kiss these glorious flowers into their pregnant fulfillment, their fruits. Verily there is nothing nobler than these fruits, which represents the bliss Absolute.

Q: Who is better: A man who strives for Self-realization (*samādhi*) or one who serves society thinking every being as a visible form of God?

A: This question is exhaustively answered in the *Īśāvāsyopaniṣad*. In the present state of the world, the tragedy of humanity is that too many people serve the world thinking that they are helping their generation. But, unfortunately, one of the curses of the world is the so-called "service" rendered by men who are unfit to serve.

Selfless dedicated service to the world in an attitude of worship is the way and the path. The greatest adoration that one can pay to his creator is to fully bring out the faculties given to him from above to the altar of service to all His creatures.

Thus, in the beginning, the seeker discovers in selfless activity a means to purify himself, whereby his mind expands to discover in it an accommodation of the whole universe of creatures. By this process, his ego, with its vanity, lust, greed, and selfishness are all removed. A mind so purified comes to manifest its powers of contemplation, and thus the seeker enhances his capacity to meditate.

Meditating under this stepped-up momentum, the person rises into new heights of self-discovery of the oneness of life, which in its turn makes him more and more a dedicated servant of mankind.

In short, true selfless actions help meditation, and successful meditation makes the meditator more and more selfless and loving. In this mutual synthesis, the seeker marches ahead into the portals of the Self, wherein he experiences what you term *samādhi*.

After this Self-realization, service of the world is not a means to an end but it is the fulfillment of the wisdom. He cannot but act, as the birds cannot but sing in the springtime. Such great men alone have ever successfully served the society. All others in the name of service pour out but death and disaster, sorrow, and destitution into the society with their so-called schemes and plans.

Why should we serve the society and the nation? Why should we share our earnings with the downtrodden? The answer, as discovered by our rishis, is because action is inevitable. We cannot keep quiet for even a moment. Every living organism must work. When we apply for casual leave and stay at home, we still do a lot of work, such as disciplining the children, quarreling with our spouse, and so on. Even when lying in bed, our mind wanders everywhere, seething with activity. When we are asleep, we are dreaming, breathing, pulsating with life. There is absolutely no escape from work. Yet we have a choice in selecting the nature of work, either good or bad. It is here that we have to exercise our faculty of discrimination.

In any society the minority produces and the majority consumes. The minority should share whatever they produce with the rest; as happens in all developed countries. All such countries were poor once; they progressed only by hard work. When a rose plant has flowers, it sheds its fragrance in all directions not expecting thanks from anybody, irrespective of whether it grows in a public garden or in the seclusion of a forest. Let the rose plant be your adviser regarding service. In the same way, do your duty without expecting any reward or publicity.

Our rishis considered the whole cosmos as one, and all things in it as limbs of this cosmos. That is what all our scriptures declare. Though all of us belong to different castes, colors, states and nations, and though we differ physically, intellectually and emotionally there is the presence of life in everybody. So when we serve others, we are merely serving ourselves! What we do to others will come back to us.

The world gives us so much, so many comforts, and so many facilities. How can we repay this debt? Whatever we may do to repay, still we will be deeply indebted to society. Our attitude should be that even if we have to suffer everyone else should be joyous. With this spirit of service, life will be full. Whatever we have must be shared with others.

Necessary Conditions for Devotion

Q: What are the three conditions necessary for devotion?

A: In verse twenty of the twelfth chapter of the *Bhagavad Gītā*, Lord Krishna points out three conditions that are absolutely necessary in order that devotion unto the Lord may yield its promised dividend.

Fixing their thought on Me. Thought is the content of our subtle body. Both the mind and intellect are nothing but thoughts. It is not sufficient if they leisurely wander around the concept of the Lord; they have to actually penetrate, delve into, merge, and ultimately dissolve themselves to become the very ideal perfection which the Lord represents. The word used here in the verse indicates not merely a thought contact but an actual thought penetration. In fact, human thought takes the form of, gathers the fragrance of, and even puts on the glow of the object's qualities in its contemplation. Thus, when a devotee's thoughts gush forward in sincerity, in a newly found urge of irrepressible love toward the Lord, the devotee, as a personality, ends for the time being, and he himself acquires the glow and beauty of the Lord of his heart.

Ever self-controlled, worship Me. The second condition necessary for a devotee to accomplish his evolution through the path of devotion is that he must have sufficient balance in himself to exercise regular self-control while worshiping the Lord. The mind, by its very nature, will always try to run away from its object of contemplation, and the art of keeping the thoughts balanced at its point of concentration is called self-control. The Sanskrit word *upāsanā*, though it translates as worship, should not suggest the superficial word "worship" that automatically comes to mind when we hear the word. True *upāsanā* is an inward act of attunement with the higher principle so as to develop ourselves to completely merge with It.

With supreme Faith. Faith is generally understood as blind belief. Blind belief is not *śraddhā*. *Śraddhā* is my belief in

45

something that I do not know, so that I may come to know that which I believe. Without developing this faculty a devotee may not succeed sufficiently in bringing about the divinity within himself, even after years of practice.

Thus, three main conditions are enumerated in this stanza as essential and unavoidable for one to become a true devotee: 1) perfect faith; 2) ever steadfast in worship and 3) one's mind totally merged with the concept of the Lord. The Lord considers anyone who accomplishes these as the most steadfast devotee.

Q: What should be the attitude of a devotee when offering gifts to the Lord?

A: An offering can be efficient only when it is accompanied by two required conditions: a) offered with devotion and b) by the pure-minded. To the extent these conditions are absent, all offerings are mere economic waste and superstition-breeding false beliefs. If properly done, it can serve as a good vehicle to tread the spiritual path of self-development.

Q: How can we remember God throughout our everyday activities?

A: Lord Krishna says in the *Bhagavad Gītā*, "Whatever you do, whatever you eat, whatever you offer in sacrifice, whatever you give, whatever you practice as austerity, O Kaunteya, do it as an offering to Me." (9:27) Through all the activities of life one can constantly live in a spirit of devout offering unto the Supreme.

Throughout, the *Bhagavad Gītā* insists time without number, that the mental attitude is of supreme importance, much more than the mere physical act. And this is a fact that ordinarily the seekers forget. All acts of perception and our reactions to the perceived, be they on the physical, mental, or intellectual levels, make them all a devout offering unto Him. In fact, this is not an unnecessary make-belief or a mere fancied exaggeration. Nor is it in any way difficult for an individual to practice. The one Self revels everywhere; in the teacher, in the devotee and in the Lord. In all our life's transactions we behave, act, and deal with other names and forms, and all of them, we know, require the existence of the Self to uphold them. To remember the Self during all transactions of life is to remember the substratum.

In a cloth shop where there are cotton clothes of different colors and sizes, textures and prices, the shopkeeper is advised always to remember that he is dealing with cotton clothing. This cannot be very difficult for any good shopkeeper, and it is safe and profitable for him to remember this fact. It thus prevents him from entertaining misconceptions and thereby either charging the exorbitant prices of woolens, or selling off his goods too cheaply! In the same way, it is only for his own benefit that a goldsmith is asked to remember that he is working on gold.

Just as cotton is in all cloth, gold in all ornaments, the Self is the Essential substance in all names and forms. A devotee who can constantly remember the Divine in all his contacts in life is alone the one who can give to life the respect and reverence that it deserves. It is a law of life that as you give unto life, so shall life give unto you. Smile at life and life smiles; frown at life and life frowns at you. Approach life with due reverence and respect, born out of cognition of the divine Essence in it, and life shall respect and revere you.

When we perform our activities in a spirit of offering, not only our love for the Supreme increases but also our entire life becomes sanctified with a noble purpose and a divine aim. In the context of the *Bhagavad Gītā's* insistence on single-pointedness of mind, and devoted contemplation of the Self, we can easily see how this stanza provides us again with an efficient and secret method by which seekers are unconsciously made to remember the Supreme constantly. Not in the deep jungles, nor in the secret caves, but right in the field of life's daily contentions.

Q: How can we reconcile the apparently conflicting ideas of self-surrender and self-assertion, the former of the *bhakta* and the latter of the *Vedāntin*?

A: The apparent conflicts need not be reconciled, the apparent has to be rejected. Self-surrender and self-assertion are merely two sides of one and the same coin. The *bhakta* surrenders his self: the ego. The *Vedāntin* asserts his Self: the Divine light within him.

Thus a devotee grows in his God-love to become ultimately a true *Vedāntin*, and a *Vedāntin* starts his career in *bhakti*. It is self-surrender alone that can evolve us to the state of self-assertion. Hence, there is no conflict at all between self-surrender and self-assertion as you suspect.

By surrendering the delusory sense of separateness, the yogi in his perfection realizes the true nature of the Self in him. The principles of self-surrender and self-assertion seem as conflicting ideas only to the novice uninitiated into the Creed of Love while it is the natural and the logical process in the noble science of *Brahamavidyā*. Negate the ego through surrender, and once this is achieved the superman so born necessarily comes to assert his divine Nature.

VII

Deepening Our Love for God

by Sri Daya Mata

The search for God begins with yearning. We must yearn for Truth, for some relationship with God. So the first quality one needs to develop is a deep, sincere longing for God, for His love.

In the beginning, you may not yet feel love for Him, but you can cultivate the desire to know Him by reflecting on how much you need Him. It has often been said that suffering is the greatest teacher. To a degree it is true that people turn to God when they have been disappointed by human beings or by the things the world has to offer. I think I was born with that—not disillusionment with people, because I love them—but the knowledge that neither the world nor any human being could give me what I wanted.

Every one of us is looking for perfection; not one of us craves anything less than perfect love, perfect relationships with others. As a young child I had the idea that such perfection was not to be found in the world. I realized I had no right to expect it of other people, because I myself am imperfect. How dare I demand from others something I myself am incapable of giving? Out of this kind of reasoning grew the desire: "Let me then begin my search for God." Only He can fully satisfy our longing, our need, for perfect love and understanding. No ordinary human being can. Having understood that God alone can fulfill our deepest needs; our desire for Him begins to unfold.

One of the first thoughts that impressed me from the scriptures was this: "Seek ye first the kingdom of God, and His righteousness, and all these things shall be added unto you." (Matthew 6:33) I kept revolving that truth in my mind. We draw many beautiful thoughts from the scriptures, and become inspired for a moment; then we forget them, without really applying them in our lives. But the scriptures are a textbook of principles that, if we live them, produce proven results as surely as do the laws of mathematics.

I decided to apply that one quotation in my life. I wanted to know whether it was true, or whether it was just a glorious statement from some exalted human being who did not really have to face the "nitty-gritty" of daily life. I kept to that one point: seek God first; then, the scripture tells me, everything else will fall into its rightful place, everything else will be added unto me. Whenever there was any kind of temptation or distraction, I held to that: seek *Him*. I proved to my own satisfaction that the truths taught and lived by the Great Ones can transform our own lives, too; for they had to face the same struggles, heartaches, and disappointments that all mankind faces.

Once a person grasps this, he will look for a way to approach God. The practice I have followed, as have many other disciples of Guruji, is simply, first of all, yearning for God; and then cultivating a personal relationship with Him through devotion.

To have an intimate relationship with God, you have to get to know Him. If you were asked to love someone you didn't know, you would find it very difficult to do so—even if told of that individual's wonderful qualities. But if you were to meet that person and spend some time with him, you would begin to know him, then to like him, and then to love him. That is the course to follow in developing love for God.

The question is, *how* to get to know Him? That is where meditation comes in. All scriptures encourage the individual who is seeking God, who wants to know Him, to sit quietly to commune with Him. In Self-Realization Fellowship we practice meditation techniques as well as chanting and prayer to achieve this. Some method is essential. You cannot know Him by reading a book about divine joy or love. Though spiritual writings do inspire fervor and faith, they do not give the end result. Nor does merely listening to a lecture about God. You must sit quietly in deep meditation, if even for just a few moments each day, taking the mind away from all else and focusing it on God alone. Thereby you gradually come to know Him; and knowing Him, you cannot help but love Him.

The Value of Group Meditation

Devotion is strengthened by association with others who are also deeply seeking God. That was the ideal on which Guruji started meditation groups and centers all over the world. He used to say, "I am not interested in building huge edifices of stone wherein God is absent. We should have many small temples filled with a true spirit of devotion for God and of united seeking of God." Groups of devotees should come together to commune with God, each the spiritual friend of the other, and each interested in serving the group as a whole.

I remember once, years ago, Guruji went to the eastern part of the United States to give classes and *Kriyā Yoga* initiation. During that period we had a service leader here who was very dry, uninteresting, boring. No inspiration came to me, so I decided not to go to the chapel any more. As I thought I did much better in my room, I would stay there and meditate.

When Guruji came back, he called me to him, and said, "I understand you are not going to meditation?"

I said, "But, Master, I am meditating." We love to rationalize, don't we? We always have seemingly logical excuses.

"But you're not going to the *chapel* any more?"

I replied, "No, I meditate better in my room; I can go much deeper. Down there, the teacher is very boring."

He said, "You go just the same. Go, not to be inspired by the teacher, but to seek deeply within yourself. Don't be dependent on anyone else; you are there for one reason, to commune with

God." I never forgot that. It was a great and wonderful lesson that has remained with me.

When you gather with others for meditation, forget everybody else. Go there just to commune with God. There is no question about it, when our own will is weak, joining a group with like interest helps to strengthen us. If you are in your own home, and there are problems to be solved, or you have had a hard day, you may say, "I won't meditate tonight. I'll just rest. Today has been really hectic." You put off meditating, and then you put it off again, because every day there is some seemingly legitimate reason. I see someone nodding his head in agreement, so you are understanding me!

When anything tries to deter you, say, "No. I must join the group for meditation." But go for the right reason, because you want to make the spiritual effort to change yourself. You are not there to impress or reform anyone else. In that meditative environment there is an exchange: others in the group give you strength, and you give them strength.

Cultivating a Personal Relationship

Do not think that you must forsake the world and enter an ashram in order to seek God. No matter how active you are, you can find time to cultivate a loving, personal relationship with Him. With my responsibilities, looking after the affairs of Guruji's society not only in this country but also in India and other parts of the world, I am as busy as the busiest of you. But God comes first. I allow nothing to interfere with that. What is necessary is yearning for God, and the willpower to make time for Him in daily meditation.

Meditation must never become for you just a routine, humdrum activity. In my travels I have gone to temples, mosques, and churches, and around the world I have seen devotees saying their prayers with distracted minds. I remember visiting the holy places in Jerusalem where Jesus Christ walked and communed with God, and seeing that the priest conducting the service was praying mechanically, more interested in his audience than in Him to whom he was praying. My inner feeling was: "No, no, no! You are here to commune with Christ!" Similarly, in temples in India, I saw priests perform their *pūjā*, busily looking at the other people all the while they were talking to God. The One to whom their prayers were addressed was not listening, because those devotees were not thinking of Him! The deep flaw in modern religion is that the One around whom it should revolve is totally forgotten in the preoccupation with what is going on externally. What Guruji taught is that when we sit for meditation, it is God with whom we have to do. Talk for even five minutes with God, letting no other distraction enter in, and you will find that your relationship with Him gradually becomes more real.

One way to develop one-pointed devotion is to chant mentally over and over again the name of God or some short thought or prayer addressed to Him. This is what India calls *japa yoga*, and the West knows it as a form of "practicing the Presence."

It is also helpful to express longing for God in a song addressed to Him—such as one of Guruji's *Cosmic Chants*. There are many beautiful love songs that can be addressed to God, even if they were not written for Him. One that Guruji liked was *The Indian Love Call*. How thrilling it is to offer such sentiments and longing, not to a human lover, but to God.

Also, read the lives of great souls, such as the life of Guruji, who was always immersed in the love of God.

A great help in awakening devotion is to think of someone you love very much, someone whose love has been an inspiration to you. Guruji thought of the love he had for his mother, which was beautiful, noble, and pure; he revered her. As you recall the love you feel for that person—your mother, for example—turn your mind and feeling to Divine Mother. "Oh, Divine Mother, I know it is You who came to me in the form of my mother." It can be a parent, husband, wife, child, or friend.

Think of the sweet quality of that individual, and when love wells up in your heart, immediately put your mind on God. Think in those moments: "This person could not love me unless You had instilled love in him." It is from God that all love comes. When you think this way, gradually you begin to cultivate love for the Love behind those you love.

During the day, whenever anyone does something to help you, always see God's hand in the bestowal of that gift. When anyone says anything kind about you, hear the voice of God behind those words. When something good or beautiful graces your life, feel that it comes from God. Relate everything in your life back to God. Think in those terms, and you will suddenly find one day, "Oh, it is He alone with whom I have to do." God is the common denominator in the lives of all human beings. He is the prime mover behind all of our activities, our greatest well-wisher and benefactor. Can there be any greater incentive to love Him and receive His love in return?

VIII

The Alchemy of Devotion

by Sogyal Rinpoche

Just as Buddha said that of all the buddhas who attained enlightenment, not one accomplished this without relying on the master, he also said: "It is only through devotion, and devotion alone, that you will realize the absolute Truth."

The absolute truth cannot be realized within the domain of the ordinary mind. And the path beyond the ordinary mind, all the great wisdom traditions have told us, is through the heart. This path of the heart is devotion.

Dilgo Khyentse Rinpoche wrote:

> There is only one way of attaining liberation and of obtaining the omniscience of enlightenment: following an authentic spiritual master. He is the guide that will help you to cross the ocean of *saṁsāra*.
>
> The sun and the moon are reflected in clear, still water instantly. Similarly, the blessings of all the buddhas are always present for those who have complete confidence in them. The sun's rays fall everywhere uniformly, but only where they are focused through a magnifying glass can they set dry grass on fire. When the all-pervading rays of the Buddha's compassion are focused through the magnifying glass of your faith and devotion, the flame of blessings blazes up in your being.

So then, it is essential to know what real devotion is. It is not mindless adoration; it is not abdication of your responsibility to yourself, nor undiscriminating following of another's personality or whim. Real devotion is an unbroken receptivity to the truth. Real devotion is rooted in an awed and reverent gratitude, but one that is lucid, grounded, and intelligent.

When the master is able to open your innermost heart; and offers you an undeniably powerful glimpse of the nature of your mind, a wave of joyful gratitude surges up in you toward the one who helped you to see, and the truth that you now realize the master embodies in his or her being, teachings, and wisdom mind. That uncontrived, genuine feeling is always rooted in repeated, undeniable, inner experience—a repeated clarity of direct recognition—and *this*, and this only, is what we call devotion, *mö gü* in Tibetan. *Mö gü* means "longing and respect": *respect* for the master, which grows deeper and deeper as you understand more and more who he or she really is, and *longing* for what he or she can introduce in you, because you have come to know that the master is your heart link with the absolute truth and the embodiment of the true nature of your mind.

Dilgo Khyentse Rinpoche tells us,

> At first this devotion may not be natural or spontaneous, so we must employ a variety of techniques to help us to achieve this. Chiefly we must always remember the excellent qualities of the teacher, especially his kindness to us. By repeatedly generating confidence, appreciation to the guru, and devotion toward him, a time will come when the mere mention of his name or the thought of him will stop all our ordinary perceptions, and we will see him as the Buddha himself.[1]

To see the master not as a human being, but as the Buddha himself, is the source of the highest blessing. For as Padmasambhava says: "Complete devotion brings complete blessing; absence of doubts brings complete success." The Tibetans know that if you relate to your teacher as a buddha, you will receive the blessing of a buddha, but if you relate to your master as a human being, you will only get the blessing of a human being. So to receive the full transformative power of the blessing of his or her teaching, the complete unfolding of its glory, you must try and unfold in yourself the richest possible kind of devotion. Only if you come to see your master as a buddha can a buddha-like teaching come through to you from your master's wisdom mind. If you cannot recognize your master as a buddha, but see him or her as a human being, the full blessing can never be there, and even the greatest teaching will leave you somewhere unreceptive.

The more I come to reflect on devotion and its place and role in the overall vision of the teachings, the more deeply I realize that it is essentially a skillful and powerful means of making us more receptive to the truth of the master's teaching. Masters themselves do not need our adoration, but seeing them as living buddhas will enable us to listen to and hear their message and to follow their instructions with the greatest possible fidelity. Devotion, then, is in one sense the most practical way of ensuring a total respect for, and therefore openness to, the teachings, as embodied by the master and transmitted through him or her. The more devoted you are, the more open you are to the teachings; the more open you are to the teachings, the more chance there is for them to penetrate your heart and mind, and so bring about a complete spiritual transformation.

So it is only by seeing your master as a living buddha that the process of transformation of yourself into a living buddha can be truly begun and truly accomplished. When your mind and heart are fully open in joy and wonder and recognition and gratitude to the mystery of the living presence of enlightenment in the master, then slowly, over many years, transmission from the master's wisdom mind and heart to yours can take place, revealing to you the full splendor of your own buddha nature, and with it the perfect splendor of the universe itself.

This most intimate relationship between disciple and master becomes a mirror, a living analogy for the disciple's relationship to life and the world in general. The master becomes the pivotal figure in a sustained practice of "pure vision," which culminates when the disciple sees directly and beyond any doubt:

the master as the living buddha, his or her every word as buddha speech, his or her mind the wisdom mind of all the buddhas, his or her every action an expression of buddha activity, the place where he or she lives as nothing less than a buddha realm, and even those around the master as a luminous display of his or her wisdom.

As these perceptions become more and more stable and actual, the inner miracle disciples have longed for over so many lives can gradually take place: They begin to see naturally that they, the universe, and all beings without exception are spontaneously pure and perfect. They are looking at last at reality with its own eyes. The master, then, *is* the path; the magical touchstone for a total transformation of the disciple's every perception.

Devotion becomes the purest, quickest, and simplest way to realize the nature of our mind and all things. As we progress in it, the process reveals itself as wonderfully interdependent: We, from our side, try continually to generate devotion, the devotion we arouse itself generates glimpses of the nature of mind, and these glimpses only enhance and deepen our devotion to the master who is inspiring us. So in the end devotion springs out of wisdom: devotion and the living experience of the nature of mind become inseparable, and inspire one another.

The teacher of Patrul Rinpoche was called Jikmé Gyalwé Nyugu. For many years he had been doing a solitary retreat in a cave in the mountains. One day when he came outside, the sun was pouring down; he gazed out into the sky and saw a cloud moving in the direction of where his master, Jikmé Lingpa, lived. The thought rose in his mind, "Over there is where my master is," and with that thought a tremendous feeling of longing and devotion surged up in him. It was so strong, so shattering, that he fainted. When Jikmé Gyalwé Nyugu came to, the entire blessing of his master's wisdom mind had been transmitted to him, and he had reached the highest stage of realization, what we call "the exhaustion of phenomenal reality."

The Stream of Blessings

Such stories about the power of devotion and the blessing of the master do not merely belong to the past. In a figure like Khandro Tsering Chodrön, the greatest woman master of our day, who was the wife of my master Jamyang Khyentse, you see very clearly what years of the deepest devotion and practice can create out of the human spirit. Her humility and beauty of heart, and the shining simplicity, modesty, and lucid, tender wisdom of her presence are honored by all Tibetans, even though she herself has tried as far as possible to remain in the background, never to push herself forward, and to live the hidden and austere life of an ancient contemplative.

Jamyang Khyentse has been the inspiration of Khandro's entire life. It was her spiritual marriage to him that transformed her from a very beautiful and slightly rebellious young woman into the radiant *dākinī*[2] that other great masters hold in the highest regard. Dilgo Khyentse Rinpoche looked to her as a "spiritual mother," and always used to say how privileged he felt that of all the Lamas she revered and loved him most deeply. Whenever he used to see Khandro, he would take her hand and tenderly caress it, and then slowly place it on his head; he knew that was the only way he could ever get Khandro to bless him.

Jamyang Khyentse gave Khandro all the teachings, and trained her and inspired her to practice. Her questions to him would be in the form of songs, and he would write songs back to her, in an almost teasing and playful way. Khandro has demonstrated her undying devotion to her master by continuing to live after his death in the place in Sikkim where he lived toward the end of his life, and where he died, and where his relics are kept, enshrined in a *stūpa*.[3] There, near him, she carries on her clear independent life, devoted to constant prayer. She has read the whole *Word of the Buddha* and hundreds of volumes of commentaries, slowly, word by word. Dilgo Khyentse Rinpoche used to say that every time he went back to the *stūpa* of Jamyang Khyentse, he felt as if he were coming home, because Khandro's presence made the atmosphere so rich and warm. It was as if, he implied, my master Jamyang Khyentse was still present and still alive, in her devotion and her being.

Again and again, I have heard Khandro say that if your link with your master is kept really pure, then everything will go well in your life. Her own life is the most moving and exquisite example of this. Devotion has enabled her to embody the heart of the teachings and radiate their warmth to others. Khandro does not teach in a formal way, in fact, she does not speak a great deal; but what she does say can often be so penetratingly clear that it becomes prophetic. To listen to her fervent and blissful chanting, or to practice with her, is to be inspired to the depths of your being. Even to walk with her, or shop, or simply sit with her is to bathe in the powerful, quiet happiness of her presence.

Because Khandro is so retiring, and because her greatness is in her ordinariness, only those with real insight see who she is. We live in a time when those who thrust themselves forward are frequently admired the most, but it is in the humble, like Khandro, that the truth really lives. And if Khandro were ever to teach in the West, she would be a perfect master: the very greatest kind of woman master, one who incarnates with a mysterious completeness the love and healing wisdom of Tara, enlightened compassion in its female form. If I were to die, and Khandro were there next to me, I would feel more confident and more at peace than if any other master were by my side.

All that I have realized I have realized through devotion to my masters. Increasingly, as I go on teaching, I become aware, humbly and with real awe, of how their blessings are beginning to work through me. I am nothing without their blessing, and if there is anything I feel I can do, it is acting as a bridge between you and them. Again and again, I notice that when I speak of my masters in my teaching, my devotion to them inspires a vision of devotion in those listening; and in those marvelous moments I feel my masters are present, blessing and opening the hearts of my students to the truth.

FOOTNOTES:

[1] Dilgo Khyentse, *The Wish-Fulfilling Jewel: The Practice of Guru Yoga According to the Longchen Nyingthig Tradition.* p. 51.
[2] A *Dākinī* is a female embodiment of enlightened energy.
[3] A *stūpa* is a three-dimensional construction symbolizing the mind of the buddhas. It often contains the relics of great masters.

IX

The Holy Mother and Simple Faith

by Swami Swahananda

[Shri Sharada Devi, the Holy Mother, was the divine consort and first disciple of Shri Ramakrishna.]

Religion is a very natural thing in a man's life. It is in his very constitution. Primitive man had a natural faith. A child also has this natural faith in everything around him. But with the development of his mind, with the acquiring of reason and knowledge, he begins to doubt. The Biblical story of Adam tasting the fruit of the tree of knowledge and his downfall which resulted is true in a sense. The high pedestal where man was in intimate relations with the higher spirit is his no more, for his ego separates him from God. The function of religion is to regain that unity. So to develop in religion is to develop this natural faith. That is why all the great teachers have advised man to return to the simplicity of a child. Says Shri Ramakrishna:

> Till one becomes simple like a child, one cannot get divine illumination. Forget all the worldly knowledge that you have acquired and become as ignorant of it as a child; then you will get the knowledge of the Truth.

There is also the well-known saying of Christ:

> Verily I say unto you, except ye be converted, and become as

little children, ye shall not enter into the kingdom of heaven. Whosoever therefore shall humble himself as this little child, the same is greatest in the kingdom of heaven.

The psychological benefit of cultivating the attitude of a child is immense. Modern man is beset with many difficulties over which he has no control. He can face them only if he has a simple faith in God applied in life situations. What we learn when we read the life and talks of the Holy Mother is this same simplicity in religion. The simple way is the way of faith and surrender. This is enough to lead the devotee gradually to the highest goal. So she said to one person: "Why are you afraid, my son? Know that the Master is ever behind you. And I am there. Don't fear as long as I am your Mother."

Religion consists of this natural relationship with God and His Incarnations. Religious life does not mean something artificial or vague or remote. It is not posing a thing that we don't have. Nor is it creating conflict in the mind by absorbing differing subtle philosophical ideas. The philosophers are there to debate the meaning or truth about them. Simple religious life does not require all this agitation. Marguerite the mystic once reproved a nun who tried to assume what she regarded as an appropriately grave exterior: "There is no sin being thought silly, but there may easily be sin in trying to look so correct. Do let yourself be natural!"

The Holy Mother too says even about a man of realization: "What else does one obtain by the realization of God? Does he grow two horns? No, his mind becomes pure, and through a pure mind one attains knowledge and awakening."

A Mother First

The Holy Mother is a mother first and a teacher next. Or it may be said that she is the mother among teachers or the teacher among mothers. Who else but a mother would waive the injunctions of the scriptures and tell her spiritual child, "My son, can a mother ever be step-motherly. You may, if you like, first eat and then begin *japa* and meditation."

The Holy Mother's religion is a religion of simple faith and surrender. Faith requires simplicity, guilelessness, and openness of mind. It is more than enough if the devotee can develop the attitude of a kitten. The kitten has absolute faith in its mother. It surrenders and depends on her totally. The only effort it makes is to cry "mew, mew." The mother cat too feels her responsibility and is all attention to the kitten. Similarly, what happens when a small boy tries to cross a busy thoroughfare? Everyone on the street feels concerned about him and tries to help him. Likewise, let us depend on God. Let us throw our burdens down right now and surrender to Him. Devotees sometimes say they have surrendered all, but they do not accept in their heart of hearts that God has taken their burdens and is leading them. That means the ego is still active and they have not yet been able to surrender totally. They must try hard to look to God and God alone and raise as few doubts as possible. Then the path will be clear and smooth. As Francois de Sales wrote once to Jeanne de Chantal, the Mother Superior of the Order of the Visitation: "Simplify your judgment. Do not have too many objections but walk simply and with confidence, do not look so much in this or that direction, but keep your eyes steadfastly focused on God and on yourself."

The Holy Mother instructed her despondent spiritual children in the same manner. All the details of why and how cannot be solved. The devotee's part is only to depend on God. Once a devotee said to the Holy Mother that he was not able to meditate. She replied, "It does not matter. It will be enough if you look at the picture of the Master."

The devotee said, "Mother, I do not succeed in regularly counting the beads three times a day." The Holy Mother's answer was, "If that is so, then think of the Master; perform your *japa* whenever you can; at least, you can salute him mentally, can't you?" This is spiritual discipline in its barest simplicity.

Burdened with the *saṁskāra* of past lives or of the present one, many devotees are not fit to practice more rigorous disciplines. So the mother in Sarada Devi guided them in the easiest way possible. This is not because these devotees will always remain at that stage. A time will come when they will begin to march more quickly. It is also true that God does not look at the amount of effort made, but sees the longing and faith of the devotee.

The Holy Mother says: "God is not like fish or vegetables that you can buy Him for a price."

And again: "You talk of having done so much *japa*, or so much work; but nothing will avail. Who can achieve anything unless Mahamaya opens the way? O creatures, surrender yourselves, just surrender yourselves. Then only will She be gracious and clear the way for you."

X

Pervasion of the Mantra

by Swami Shraddhananda

The *mantra*[1], the Holy Name of God, received from the spiritual teacher is one with the deity. It is believed that there is no difference between the deity and His Name. This faith, though initially weak, gathers strength as the spiritual seeker goes on practicing *mantra-japa*. In the beginning, the taste for the practice may not be very deep. It seems to be a sort of mechanical enterprise, but if the aspirant does not give up and continues to repeat the mantra as instructed, the mantra becomes more and more "awakened." It removes the evil tendencies of the mind and gradually fills it with the pure joy and consciousness of God. The light of the mantra begins to illumine the heart, which is slowly raised to higher levels of spiritual reality. One such level can be called the pervasion of the mantra.

One who has received initiation from an illumined teacher keeps the mantra in his heart as a precious treasure. The initiated should not be asked by his curious friends and companions about the deity and the mantra he has received. It is an entirely private matter. During the time of contemplation the spiritual aspirant brings out from the depths of his heart the mantra, which is his precious treasure. He goes on repeating the mantra almost inaudibly or silently, with as much faith and love as possible. This technique, as we know, is called *japa*, and the expression, *japa-siddhiḥ*, perfection through *japa*, is well known among spiritual seekers. If *japa* is continued with patience and faith it is sure to reveal the truth of the deity. The scriptures and the teachings of enlightened devotees tell us that in order that the mantra is raised to the level of enlightening power, three things are essential, namely, purity of body and mind, eagerness for the vision of God, and detachment from sense-pleasure. Here are some of Shri Ramakrishna's sayings about the mantra:

> Yes, there is no doubt about the sanctity of God's name. But can a mere name achieve anything, without the yearning love of the devotee behind it? One should feel great restlessness of soul for vision of God. Suppose a man repeats the name of God mechanically, while his mind is absorbed in woman and gold. Can he achieve anything?[2]

> One attains God through *japa*. By repeating the name of God secretly and in solitude one receives divine grace then comes His vision.[3]

> Why is the name a trifling thing? God is not different from His name. Satyabhama tried to balance Krishna with gold and precious stones but could not do it. Then Rukmini put a tulsi-leaf with the name of Krishna on the scales. That balanced the Lord.[4]

We say God is *Sat-Cit-Ānanda*. Whatever exists, whatever comes to our knowledge, and whatever is joyful, inheres in God. He is *Sat* because there is no break in His existence. He is *Cit* because there is no limit to His knowledge. He is *Ānanda* or bliss, because all that is dear and loveable has its source in Him. The aspirant who is practicing *japa* has to feel that, like God, the Holy Name also is *Sat-Cit-Ānanda*. It is the desire of the aspirant that during *japa* his limited existence may enter the unlimited existence of *Śabda Brahman* (*Brahman* as sound), and his heart may be filled with the blissful, spiritual light of the mantra. This desire cannot, of course, be fulfilled in one day. One has to carry on spiritual practices with patience, hope, and faith. Then the time comes when God as the mantra becomes fully awakened.

The awakened mantra cannot be kept concealed in the throat or in the heart. The mantra begins to expand. When there is a flood, the waters of the river overflow the banks and spread far and wide. In the same manner, the awakened mantra is felt as emerging not merely from the lips or tongue or throat, but from everywhere.

A Divine Body

Expansion of the mantra involves the spiritual transformation of the object, which is touched by the mantra. Here are some examples. Through our physical eyes we see numerous objects. Let the mantra be directed to the eyes. Wherever the eyes now turn, the glow of the Spirit radiates from the object seen. The visual experience then will seem to be the sound of the mantra. Whatever visual knowledge comes through the eyes is now equivalent to the repetition of the mantra. When *japa* was done through the throat or mentally, the mantra was nothing but a subtle sound. Now that sound has been transformed into form. The seeker sees all the patterns that are floating in the mind as the expression of the mantra. The mantra-consciousness is thus extended to all forms seen by the eyes.

The physical ears, by the touch of the mantra, become transformed into "divine ears." Whatever sounds enter into those ears are not ordinary sounds. They are the vibrations of the mantra. Thus sang Ramprasad: "Whatever you hear with your ears is the Name of the Mother. Mother manifests through fifty letters and these create Her endless Names."

Similarly the three other sense organs namely, those of touch, smell, and taste become companions of *mantra-japa* when enlivened by the mantra-consciousness. All experiences of touch, smell, and taste bring the joy and satisfaction of *mantra-japa*. In the same way, any other part of the body, besides the sense organs, can be spiritualized by the expansion of the mantra. The heartbeat, the breathing process of the lungs, the circulation of blood, the flow of nerve currents, all of these can be experienced as the play of the mantra. The mantra goes on working in every segment of the body. In one word, all the vital activities of the body participate in *mantra-japa*.

The inner organ (*antaḥkaraṇa*) with its four limbs—namely, mind (*manas*), memory (*citta*), determinative faculty (*buddhi*), and ego, (*ahaṅkāra*)—do not stand idle. They also participate in the *japa* done by the spiritual seeker. To him whatever waves arise in the mind are a representation of the mantra. Any definite ascertainment by the *buddhi* appears to the seeker to be the revelation of the mantra. The ego gives up its assertion of individuality and becomes a spiritualized expression of the mantra.

The pervasion of the body, mind and *prāṇa* by the mantra is not a matter of little blessing. Shri Ramakrishna used to say that the body of a devotee is the playground of consciousness. When the seeker carries on his *japa* with faith, love, and patience, his psychophysical system becomes a "divine body." Heaven, as it were, descends into that body. The *Kena Upaniṣad* (2:4) points this out when it says: "One attains immortality when the Self is known in every piece of cognition."

If it is true that the mantra received from the teacher is verily *Śabda Brahman* (*Brahman* as sound), then it is but natural that its expansion will go on even outside the body-mind complex. The Upanishads say that *Brahman* is all-pervasive, all-penetrating. The *mantra-sādhaka*, in the same manner, wants to realize that the mantra too is all-pervading. This is one positive step toward Self-knowledge. The seeker directs his mantra towards the sky and says, "O sky, the leader of the five elements, who are, in fact, consciousness revealed to me that way, be one with my mantra. I want to hear the unstruck (*anāhata*) sound of the mantra in your vast reality." In the same manner, when the mantra is experienced in the second element, *vāyu* (air), the seeker experiences the divine dance of the mantra in the gentle breeze, strong wind, as also in the terrible storm.

By deep contemplation, the other three elements—namely, *teja* (energy), *āpaḥ* (water), and *kṣiti* (earth)—are similarly transformed into mantra. In fact, any kind of energy considered from the spiritual perspective is grasped as the unfoldment of the mantra. We encounter water in so many different forms: as rain, mist, cloud, ice, waterfall, river, seas, ocean. The *mantra-sādhaka* tries to feel all these water-forms as his mantra. Now comes the fifth element, *kṣiti* (earth). Extensive green grain-fields, vines, bushes, trees, as also dreary deserts, hills, and mountains, all these, are various forms of the fifth element, earth. However soft or hard, however small or big, into each of these forms the mantra has the power to enter. In the experience of the seeker, all these forms merge into one unified, homogeneous consciousness.

The Upanishads and the *Bhagavad Gītā* have described the all-pervasiveness and all-inclusiveness of the Supreme Spirit. There is not even a single object or event where the consciousness of the Supreme Self is absent. If the mantra is the Sound of *Brahman*, if the *nāma* (name) is one with the *nāmī* (one possessing the name), then the *Iṣṭa-mantra* too is really all-extensive and all-embracing.

By the grace of God and the Guru, fortunate spiritual aspirants can feel the pervasion of the mantra from time to time during the practice of *japa*. Let us remember a passage from the *Māṇḍūkya Upaniṣad*: "*Om* is all this. All that is past, present and future is, indeed, *Oṅkāra*. And whatever else there is beyond the three levels of time is also *Oṅkāra*."

These are not empty words. The illumined sages of the past, as well as many spiritual aspirants, men and women of later times, have realized the truth of this statement. Whatever the Vedas have spoken about *Oṅkāra* is also true in the case of various *Iṣṭa-mantra* of the *Tāntrika* and *Paurāṇika* deities. Receiving the *Siddha-mantra* from an illumined teacher, if we go on practicing *japa* with love and patience, then the mantra soon becomes "awakened" and pervades the body, mind, *prāṇa*, as also our actions, and floods the world around us. Our spiritual life then becomes blessed to the utmost.

FOOTNOTES:

[1] Since this word is used repeatedly throughout the text, we have italicized only the first use and have used roman for subsequent occurrences.

[2] *The Gospel of Shri Ramakrishna*, p. 190

[3] Ibid., p. 588

[4] Ibid., p. 386

XI

A Dialogue with Jean Vanier

Edited by Tim Kearney

Tim Kearney: You have a deep conviction of the ways in which people with learning disabilities can be prophetic. But is this not something of a generalization? Could you say more about this?

Jean Vanier: I would like to speak in wider terms, about how people with disabilities can change us, open our hearts and call us to new ways of living.

It is like a businessman or a banker who has to be efficient. He works all day long with computers or figures, gives orders or has to make important decisions. When he comes home at night, he can be so tired that he just sits down in front of the television and does not want to be bothered. Or else he can come home to his children, listen to them and talk to them, get down on his hands and knees and play with them. He is a different man! His children call forth something else in him, another part of his being! It is the same way with people who are weak or old or sick or disabled. They call out the child, the tenderness and compassion in us. In that way people with disabilities are prophetic; they have a secret power to change people's hearts and to make us more human.

I remember when I was invited to speak to the theology students at Harvard University. They asked me to talk to them about people with disabilities. I began by reading from the book of Isaiah: "Who can believe what we have heard? A man of sorrow, familiar with suffering... he had no form or charm to attract us, no beauty to win our hearts ... *and yet it is by his wounds that we are healed."* (Is. 53).

I told them that many of the people I was living with did not know how to read or write or even speak, and yet many of them had a deeper experience of Jesus than they, the students, had. I told them: "You are looking for a *knowledge* of Jesus whereas people with learning disabilities are seeking a *presence* of Jesus; their intellectual capacity for words and concepts is greatly limited, but their intuition, their sense of presence is greatly increased."

So, people with disabilities can bring us to what is most essential in Christianity. Christianity is centered on a person, the person of Jesus, the presence of Jesus, who reveals to us that we are loved and who calls us, in turn, to love. There is a double movement: God loves us and calls us to love others; we are called to drink from the source in order to become a source.

Tim Kearney: So what do people with learning disabilities teach us in this sense?

Jean Vanier: They remind us that what is essential is this personal, heart-to-heart relationship with Jesus. I often quote John the Evangelist in his first letter: *Beloved, let us love one another, because love is from God and whoever loves is born of God and knows God.* (I John 4) In biblical language "to know" God means "to have an experience" of God. People with disabilities are teaching us something about the importance of presence and of relationship.

Let me tell you a lovely story that shows this prophetic element of people with learning disabilities. A young boy with a mental handicap was making his First Communion. There was a beautiful liturgy followed by a family celebration.

During the family gathering the uncle turns to the mother and says: "Wasn't that a beautiful liturgy, the only sad thing is that the little boy understood nothing!" With tears in his eyes, the boy says: "Don't worry Mummy, Jesus loves me just as I am."

73

So there you see the realization of Paul's words, that "God has chosen the foolish and the weak to confound the wise and the strong." The uncle had not really understood. The little boy, in some way, was prophetic.

Importance of Relationships

Tim Kearney: In your life in your community in Trosly, are there any particular people who you would like to cite as having been important for you in that sense?

Jean Vanier: I would mention Raphael Simi and Philippe Seux, the first two men I welcomed in L'Arche. I came from a naval career where I had been taught to be quick and efficient. Then I did several years of intense study and began a doctorate. That implied a great deal of intellectual work. There was something lacking, however, in terms of relationship. I was more a man of action and of teaching. As I began to share my life with Raphael and Philippe and we did things together, I began to change.

Tim Kearney: In what way did they call you to change?

Jean Vanier: They showed me the importance of *being with* others, of entering into relationship, friendship with others, of "wasting time" together, sharing meals and laughter. They brought out what I would call the "playfulness" of the child in me.

Through their simplicity, their joking, their need for friendship, they were forming my heart and calling forth tenderness and compassion in me. But they also revealed the anger in me. Because as soon as we start lowering the barriers around our hearts and our defense mechanism, other feelings can emerge, such as anger or violence. Raphael and Philippe touched and called forth in me what was most beautiful, the capacity to relate, to be sensitive to others and to have fun together, but they also brought me in contact with my capacity to hurt, my difficulties in relationship, and my own inner brokenness.

Tim Kearney: In revealing to you your limits and your shadow side, as you were describing there—your brokenness—was that important for you as a point of growth in your own journey?

Jean Vanier: As I look back in retrospect, I would say yes, but at the moment itself, no. Because it is painful to touch one's anger and violence; it seems to go against our vocation to love and to be close to people, especially those who are weak and poor. A sense of guilt can arise. But this led me to a greater awareness of who I really was. As I gradually discovered my "shadow side," I realized that I had to work at it and learn how to live through it. Then, what I realized more than anything else was how much I needed Jesus and the Holy Spirit.

Not just psychological help but I needed a power of the Spirit to discover that I did not have to live just from my "woundedness," but that I could also live from the light that is in me. At that time, I discovered a letter Carl Jung had written to a Christian woman. Referring to the text in Matthew (25:31-46), he expressed his admiration of Christians who saw a real presence of Jesus in the poor: "I admire you Christians, because when you see somebody hungry or thirsty, you see Jesus in them. When you visit a prisoner or the sick, when you see someone naked or somebody strange, you see Jesus in them." Then he goes on, "What astonishes me, is that you do not see Jesus in your own poverty, hunger, and thirst. Don't you realize that you too are imprisoned, in your own fears? Don't you see that you too are sick and that there are strange things inside of you that you don't understand, and that in some way you are naked?"

This text helped me to realize that we all have to work at befriending our shadow side in order to grow. I also began to realize that one of the greatest fears of human beings is to kill someone in a fit of anger. Perhaps that is why we create walls of prejudice in order to prevent ourselves from harming or killing another person. As I mentioned before, we create walls of prejudice that say, "these people are no good." Then we don't have to have any contact with them; we can separate ourselves from them and thus the danger of killing them is minimized. I'm beginning to see more and more how prejudices are a part of our protective mechanism, and how they have to be broken down in order to find our source and in order to let what I would call our "deeper self" emerge.

Love: Our Priority

Tim Kearney: Looking at the Christian Churches in the world today, at the beginning of a new millenium, what, in your view, is their greatest challenge?

Jean Vanier: I sense so much chaos in our world in many different areas: the immense discrepancy between the rich and the poor, the development of armaments and the links between economy and armaments, the developments in genetics, the widespread breakdown of human relationships, just to give a few examples. Then there is the influence of television, which is like a powerful teacher right there in the home. It teaches a lot about violence and sexuality, which a young person usually integrates into his or her life in the context of family. Sexuality and violence touch what I call the chaotic energies within us. So there is something new happening and a whole breakdown of the "old."

What is the reaction of the Churches confronted with this situation? On the one hand, there is the reaction of: "We must get together and create strong groups and provide a formative education in order to protect Christian rules and regulations." This gives birth to strong, rigid, sometimes almost "sectarian" groups in the Churches. On the other hand, there is a Christianity that is falling into a "Gallup poll" mentality: if you have enough people saying that something should be done, then that justifies it. There is an absence of any sense of authority except perhaps that Jesus had something to say and that it was important.

Yet Jesus himself was at times quite clear and strong in the way he exercised authority. So, we are falling either into an absence of any authority where everybody feels that they have the truth and can do what they want, or else into protecting ourselves behind the rules of a rather rigid, blind authoritarianism.

My hope is that, just as the Spirit of God hovered over the chaos at the beginning of the creation of the world, so too, as we experience the breakdown of society today, the Spirit of God is there and new life is already emerging within our world and within the Churches. There can be a danger in our Churches of putting structure, morality, and dogma before love. But love is our priority. We have to come back to the words of Paul: "If you have all the languages, if you have faith that can move mountains [which is pretty good!], if you give all your goods to the poor and if you give your body to the flames, but do not have love, then, all that counts for nothing." (I Cor. 13:3)

What is this love? It comes back to heart-to-heart relationships. Relationships that reveal to others their beauty. A love that brings people together, not to a place of intellectual security or power, but to a place of service and unity. As I was saying before, it is often those who are in need who can bring us to this place, to the heart.

Some seminarians, after years of studies, having gone through seminary, and in some cases having obtained a doctorate in canon law, can be so very weak in the area of relationships. They are frightened of relationships, and of the heart, and even frightened of love, because relationships can be linked to sexuality, which causes a deep fear.

One way of helping people to integrate their sexuality, and their hearts, and to become men and women of relationship, is the experience of one-to-one relationships with someone who is weak, elderly, ill or dying. They call forth in us kindness, compassion and tenderness; they can teach us how to listen. They can heal us.

Tim Kearney: So somewhere there is a need for healing?

Jean Vanier: Yes, healing is necessary. In the Middle Ages, there wasn't this terrible breakdown of the family and of society.

People were quite structured relationship-wise. What they needed most, at that time, was a formation of the intellect. Today the greatest need is a healing of the affectivity. I'm not saying that intellectual formation is not necessary, it is vital. But there is a more fundamental need of healing because our hearts have been deeply wounded. Healing of the heart takes place through compassion, and the discovery that we are valued and loved, not for what we do, achieve or have, but for *who we are*. That is where Jesus is essentially the healer, saying to each person, *You are important, you are loved.*

I often quote the text of Isaiah where God says, *Do not be afraid because I have liberated you. I've called you by your name and you are mine. If you pass through the waters you will not be overwhelmed, if you pass through fire you will not be burned, because I am the Lord God of Israel, your savior, and you are precious in my eyes and I love you.* (Is. 43) Jesus reveals to each one of us that we are beautiful. As we realize that we are loved and valued by God, we want to respond to this love because love calls forth love.

What I have discovered in my life in L'Arche and through the Gospels is that our most fundamental place of belonging is not to this or that country, culture or religion, but to the human family. Whatever our religion, country or culture, whatever our gifts or limits may be, we are all precious to God.

Tim Kearney: What, in your view, is the core value of Christian spirituality?

Jean Vanier: For a Christian, spirituality is the way we are called to become one with Jesus, and through him, one with the Father and with each other, each one according to his or her gifts and vocation. To become one with Jesus means to see the world, ourselves, other people, especially the weak and the forgotten, as he sees them. To love them as he loves them. This implies a rebirth in the Spirit, a transformation of our hearts of stone into hearts of flesh.

The path on which we are called is given in the eight Beatitudes of Matthew's Gospel, which are the Charter of our lives as followers of Jesus. This means becoming less governed by our own fears, prejudices and our need to be powerful, loved and admired by others, and more governed by the gifts of the Holy Spirit and the presence of Jesus within us.

XII

Longing and Belonging

by Swami Viprananda

Longing is extolled in all religions as a prerequisite for God-realization. Shri Ramakrishna used to say, "Pray with real longing and God can't help but reveal Himself." He used to tell a story about a disciple who asked his teacher to explain the nature of longing to him. The teacher took him to a river, and the two of them waded in. Suddenly he grabbed the disciple by the top of the head and pushed him under the water. As he held him there, the disciple began thrashing his arms wildly, trying to get free. When the teacher let him up, he asked, "How did you feel?" The disciple said, "I was longing for a breath of air." "That is what real longing for God is like," his teacher replied. "When you have that kind of longing, you possess real longing."

Such longing as this is difficult to come by, no doubt. Shri Ramakrishna said that when one has this kind of longing, it means that the realization of God is not far off. He compared it to the rosy horizon, just before daybreak. On seeing it one knows that the sun is about to rise.

Many of us have struggled for years to deepen our spiritual life. We have practiced spiritual disciplines like meditation, *japa*, the reading of sacred scriptures, and the keeping of holy company. We have persevered amidst trials and tribulations. Sometimes we seem to have been making progress, while at other times we seem to have hit a dead end. In spite of our efforts, our longing for God has not grown dramatically or rapidly.

There may be various reasons for this, for instance, lingering desires for worldly enjoyment, attachments and egotism. But there may also be another contributing factor which we have not considered: we may not have a strong sense of identification with our ideal, it may not seem very close to us, nor we to it. It may not be an ideal to which we have a personal sense of belonging. So along with our spiritual practices it is also important to establish an identity with our ideal. We need to feel close to it, for unless we do, we will always feel that, in spite of our efforts, we are not making the progress we had hoped for. Thus there is a very close relationship between *longing* and a sense of *belonging*.

Getting Acquainted

Every deep human relationship involves several succeeding states: the introduction, getting acquainted, emotional bonding, intimacy, trust, and so on. The same is true for our relationship with the Divine. We cannot love what we do not know; loving implies knowing. How does this process of getting acquainted begin?

Very often the initial impetus for living a spiritual life comes from our own inner dissatisfaction and unhappiness. These two arise because of a crisis—a bereavement or illness, advancing age, a setback in financial affairs. At such a juncture we begin to suspect that something is missing from our life, that it does not satisfy us at a deeper level. If we are fortunate, we may somehow learn of a spiritual ideal that we find meaningful. We are drawn to it and begin to think about it more and more. It is then that we probably begin to see that there is a wide gulf between our life and that ideal. We realize, "I am here, and the ideal is way over there."

We then begin to see the need to change in fundamental ways in order to bridge this gulf. So we make efforts to reform our life and bring it into greater harmony with the ideal. We try to cultivate good, healthy habits of living, we try to keep holy company, and we try to give up negativity.

Perhaps at the same time, or soon thereafter, we see the need not only to reform our life but also to practice spiritual disciplines. We then become enthusiastic about practicing meditation, *japa* and prayer, reading holy books, and going to the temple or church. We may become so ardent that we even become somewhat intolerant of others who don't share our newfound enthusiasm. "Why don't they open their eyes and see how beautiful this is?" we think.

At this stage it may seem to us that everything is going along rather smoothly, with evident progress being made. Old ways of living are being given up; new habits are being cultivated. We make friends with spiritually-minded people. It is a very beautiful time in our life—the rosy horizon before the dawn, we may even think.

However, much to our consternation and distress, we find sooner or later that this stage does not last. Our spiritual practices begin to grow wearisome, our ardor begins to wane, and our mind becomes restless. We are like a married person who, having first tasted the sweetness of falling in love, eventually experiences the letdown that the reality of married life brings.

Thus we may now begin to go through periods of dryness. This wasn't supposed to happen. Everything was supposed to go along smoothly—after all, wasn't this the rosy horizon before the dawn? And so our initial enthusiasm is replaced by the realization that we are still very far from the ideal. In fact, it may seem that we are farther from it now than when we started. What a cruel psychological trick the mind sometimes plays on us: "Oh, I am not making any progress at all! I can see how spiritual other people are becoming. I look at them! They are happy, smiling, content—and they are real meditators! I can't meditate very long. My knees ache, my mind wanders. But I can see how much progress others are making!"

So our resolve begins to weaken and we begin to experience the same old tendencies we thought we had given up once and for all. They hadn't really gone anywhere; they were only biding their time, waiting for their opportunity to resurface. Shri

Ramakrishna used to say that a bath in the Ganges is purifying, as one prepares to step into the water, the person's sins fly off and perch on the tree on the bank. When the person gets out, they fly down and settle on his or her shoulder again. In the same way, even after trying for some time to live a spiritual life, we find that the seeds of the old desires, impulses, ways of thinking and living, bad habits, and so on, are still there. They haven't really been sublimated they have only been suppressed. And it will probably take a long time to eradicate them completely. This can be a very trying and painful period in our life, as we experience alternating glimmers of hope and periods of despair. For many people, spiritual life is indeed a kind of roller-coaster ride.

There is a reason for these vacillations of the mind: it is impure, it has not yet found its spiritual center. As a consequence, it is not integrated. It is ruled by subconscious desires and egoistic notions. These make it restless and unsteady. It is also true that as we undertake spiritual disciplines the subconscious mind becomes more stimulated. Spiritual practices flush out the latent desires, impulses and impressions hidden there. This can be very painful if we do not possess a strong degree of detachment. It is like pouring water into an ink well to cleanse it. As we pour in clear water, all the old, dirty ink is flushed out.

Laziness is also a problem that must be dealt with. It is human nature, as well as physical nature, to seek out a position of rest. Spiritual life, however, is like swimming upstream; it requires a great deal of effort. Laziness can also be due to a lack of deep faith.

Belonging

There is another very important reason, one that may be overlooked, why we may ride the spiritual roller-coaster of flagging efforts and dubious results: we may not feel very close to our ideal, we may not feel that we belong to it and it to us. The closer we feel to our ideal, the more centered in it our mind becomes. The more we feel a sense of belonging to our ideal, the more we are able to lead a balanced, disciplined, dynamic, creative spiritual life. When we feel a deep sense of belonging, we are less affected by the ups and downs of spiritual struggle. So how do we develop closeness? How do we feel that the divine is truly our own?

The divine reality is a stranger because we, as embodied human beings, are programmed to interact with the world and our own body in terms of the senses. Our senses lead us outward; they make us identify with the body and with the world of the senses. Being enmeshed in a world of sense life, we are estranged from the divine life within ourselves.

In order to develop closeness to our ideal, we must begin to look at ourselves in a new light. Just as we become intimate with our family and friends, so must we become intimate with our ideal. Longing deepens when we begin to feel closeness, and closeness deepens when we begin to feel longing. They are really part and parcel of the same phenomenon of spiritual growth.

There are two psychological laws that may be applied here. The first is: that becomes most meaningful to us which affects us personally. For instance, parents love their children; they feel a sense of identity with them. Their children belong to them, and they belong to their children. There is a reciprocal relationship based upon a feeling of identity or personal closeness. These same parents don't normally love others' children in the same way, though they may care for them because that sense of closeness does not expand to the same degree. Of course, there are exceptions to the rule, but these are invariably people who have become so imbued with their spiritual ideal that it has rooted outward feelings of separateness from others.

The second psychological law is: like attracts like. It is common for people of similar natures or interests to be drawn toward one another; for instance, musicians, artists, political buffs, or sports enthusiasts. This "like" also has an important application in regard to our own inner spiritual life. In order to develop closeness to our ideal, we have to establish a personal relationship based on our *likeness* to it.

What this means is that we must begin to see ourselves as expressions of divinity. This has its own unique problems, however, it is not as simple as developing closeness to other people or objects. All of us are creatures of the world. Our body is common to the material world, our persona is common to humanity, and even our thoughts generally are along predictable lines. But the divine Reality cannot be experienced in the same way, as it cannot be heard, seen, smelled, tasted or touched. It is not experienced at all, or so it would seem. How then can we establish a personal relationship with that which is beyond apprehension and comprehension?

I often think that the divine is a good listener, but not much of a talker. It is difficult to carry on a conversation with it, and it also makes the establishing of an intimate relationship a unique undertaking that requires dynamic creativity, a good measure of detachment and a lot of practice.

Nearer My God To Me

What is our likeness to the divine? A lot more than we think, although we will have to dig for it a little. Think of your own existence. What is it? Perhaps you begin by identifying yourself with your body. "This is my body," you say. "I was born on such and such a date." But if it is your body, how can it be you? It is *yours*, it is not *you*. This may seem like a moot point, but it is a very important distinction. Whatever is an object cannot be the subject, the real you. Moreover, science tells us that all the cells, molecules and atoms of our bodies are continually being replaced by new ones borrowed from someone or something else. The universe is in fact a cosmic swapmeet. We have so many borrowed parts (all of them!) that we would surely be in a state of acute identity crisis if we were really the body.

So what gives us the sense of continuity from the day we were born up to the present? Perhaps it is the mind, we may think. We say, "These are my thoughts." From this statement it is clear that we do not really believe that we are the thoughts, for we say that the thoughts are *mine*, not that they are *me*. The fact is that we witness our thoughts, just as we witness our bodies.

When we identify ourselves with the body and mind, we falsely take the objects to be the subject. This leads to fantastic conclusions like "I am fat," "I am thin," "I am young," "I am old," "I am clever," or "I am stupid." It also leads us to believe, "There is nothing about me that is spiritual," or "I am very far from the divine."

To begin to identify ourselves with the witness of the body and mind is to begin to find our likeness to the divine. What is that witness? It is pure Consciousness, the substratum of our mind. But Consciousness is impossible to understand in an objective, analytical sense. This is because it cannot be objectified; it is the eternal subject. Can anyone say what his Consciousness is? Or where it begins or ends? Can it be defined or circumscribed? Does it have any color or form? Try to see the limits of your Consciousness. Focus on it and you will see that anything that appears in consciousness is not consciousness.

Consciousness is one. It is not that you have one consciousness and I another. There is only one Consciousness, which appears to be divided into subject and object. This is a deep mystery that cannot be explained by analogy. Fortunately, the sages say that it can be realized intuitively in the depths of meditation.

Our likeness to the divine can also be understood by analyzing the nature of spiritual love. There are various levels of love, from base emotional feelings to family attachments to selfless service of all beings. One thing is common to them all: identification. The lower the level of love, the more limited and self-centered is the identification. The higher the level of love, the more universal and selfless is the identification. At the highest level, love is independent of all objects of love; it is nothing less than the unbroken awareness of unity. This is because it is the divine Reality itself. And, again, this is our likeness to the divine. As we grow spiritually, we don't have to look for love: we become love. And we then find that love pervades everything else as well.

Thus, our likeness to the divine is an incorruptible truth, however little we may be aware of it at present. And it is *intensely* personal, for it is that which is the Person of our person, the Self of our self.

Setting Up the Altar

All spiritual practices are creative when followed regularly and systematically. Their purpose is to affect a transformation in our consciousness, releasing us from the false identification with the body, mind, and ego. This may be easy to understand theoretically, but because of the persistent, overpowering illusion of our separateness from the divine and the tenacious pull of the senses, it is difficult to achieve practically. Therefore, it is often helpful to incorporate some practical aids into our spiritual disciplines. Resourcefulness can help in fixing our attention on our likeness to the divine.

There are various attitudes and disciplines we can incorporate into our spiritual life. The particular practice I have in mind, however, involves a combination of meditation, discrimination, devotion, and visualization. To counteract our identification with the body and mind, it is beneficial to look upon the body as the temple of God, who dwells in the altar of our heart, and our thoughts as the light emanating from that altar. Thus, our very life-breath is the breath of the divine breathing through us. The movements of our limbs are the dynamic power of the divine flowing through us. Our thoughts are the divine radiance. When all other beings are also seen as temples of God, our service to them becomes service of the divine.

There is a beautiful song of the Bengali saint, Ramprasad, which Shri Ramakrishna used to sing, "O my mind, worship Kali in any way thou pleasest, uttering the mantra given by the guru day and night. Know thy lying down as obeisance to Her, and meditate on Mother even while thou art asleep. O, while thou roamest a town, think that thou walkest around Mother Kali. All sounds thou hearest are her mantras." Kali is made of fifty letters (the letters of the Bengali alphabet) and She bears her name in every letter. Ramprasad says in wonder, "The Divine Mother is in every creature. O, while thou eatest, think thou offerest an oblation to Her."

This practice can be directed toward a personal aspect of God or toward the impersonal, all-pervading Existence. But it is important that the altar be consecrated daily through meditation in the heart. By visualizing the divine presence there and offering Oneself to it, in time one can make this practice true worship, in which worshiper and worshiped become one.

Moreover, once we have installed the divine in our heart, we never need feel that we are separated from it. We can carry it with us at all times and under all circumstances. Whenever life becomes difficult and we feel worried or anxious, we can remind ourselves, "Yes, the temple is here. It is very close. It is the closest of the close." Just to stop and take one moment to reflect on this fact is enough to change one's whole outlook for the day because it is truth, it is our real nature. If we consecrate our life every day in this way, we begin to see the truth of it more and more. In time we begin to have a real sense of closeness to the divine within us. This practice is very simple and very direct: install the divine in your heart and remember that *there* is where you should look at all times. And reinforce this practice as strongly as possible through meditation, prayer, reflection of your true nature, and service as worship.

The problem in developing longing for God is essentially a problem of seeing ourselves as a spiritual being. When we become aware of our spiritual nature, longing comes automatically. Thinking about something breeds attachment to it, so we must think about the divine more and more. And what better way to think of it than as the Reality within us? When we have a sense of personal identification with it, all the major obstacles are practically overcome.

Developing an awareness of the divine within us is no small achievement. It is a milestone in spiritual life. It is the beginning of the dawn of God-realization. And it is something we should long for with all our heart. Swami Prabhavananda used to say, "Long for God!" someone answered, "But I don't feel any longing for God!" he would say, "Then long for longing for God." When we attain that longing and sense of closeness to the divine, all the hard work will have been done, and we very quickly reach our goal.

PART THREE

Surrender Unto Him

*Self-Surrender is an attitude of mind,
which one acquires through the consciousness
that one's soul is a part of the Cosmic soul
and that one's body and mind
are instruments of a higher Power.*

Swami Yatiswarananda

What can we know of God with our little brain? Nothing. Therefore I ask you to surrender yourself completely to Him. His will be done. He is omnipotent! What power has man? All that you can do is to love God. Have intense yearning for Him. The whole world is mad for something; why run mad after fleeting objects of this world? Better be mad for God. The goal is to realize God. Work can never be the aim of life. Even selfless work is not an end in itself but only a means to Divine realization.

Swami Brahmananda
The Eternal Companion

When we come to know of our helpless finitude, we pray for His mercy and say, "Thy will be done," and that is what we call *śaraṇāgati* or complete surrender. *Śaraṇāgati* is that state when we give up all confidence in ourselves and completely depend on Him and give ourselves up to Him. Not even a little vanity should then remain within us. If we can renounce all our vanity and pride and humbly submit ourselves to Him, then our finite mind can feel His grace and become one with His infinity.

Swami Bhuteshananda
Thoughts on Spiritual Life

XIII

Self-Surrender

by Swami Yatiswarananda

Spiritual life is meant only for the strong. However, by strength we mean not only physical strength but also mental strength and spiritual strength. By the exercise of willpower and practice of austerity one gains tremendous inner strength. But apart from all these there is another strength—the strength of the Divine. The true devotee feels that he is under the protecting care of the almighty Divine and he feels infinite strength. Surdas, one of the great North Indian saints of the Middle Ages, sang: "By the grace of the Divine Youth of Brindavan I have understood that Rama is the strength of the weak."

Self-surrender to the Divine is in itself a mighty form of *sādhanā*. It is not as easy as people think. What people generally can do is to pray to God and depend on Him at different times of the day, and offer their body, mind and soul at the feet of the *Iṣṭa-devatā* repeatedly.

In the *Bhagavad Gītā* Lord Krishna tells Arjuna:

The Lord dwells in the hearts of all beings; and by His *māyā* causes them to turn round and round as though mounted on a machine (just as a puppet-player moves the puppets.)

Take refuge in Him with all thy heart; by His grace shalt thou attain supreme Peace and Eternal Abode. Thus has the profoundest wisdom been declared to thee by Me. Reflect over it fully and act as you like.[1]

When we draw ourselves away from Him, we become more egocentric and fall from the higher path. Instead of taking our stand on the ego, let us surrender to the Divine and make Him the center of our consciousness. And then ethical and spiritual life becomes easy. We should practice prayer, intense prayer, when lower tendencies come up. And then we will find some power coming and lifting us up.

The Blessing of Uncertainty

From a spiritual point of view it is good to remain amidst great uncertainty. It is often good if everything you relied upon is taken away from you and you are left without any worldly support. It is good if all old values, friendships, and attachments are broken, and you find all that you had clung to disappearing into the blue. It is good that all forms of external consolation, all hopes in other people, crumble. For then you will be forced to turn to the Divine, who alone is our eternal and only true Friend and Guide.

This experience is very painful, but for many people it is very necessary. Otherwise they forget God and their own spiritual destiny. You do not know anything about your own future. You cannot rely on perishable things. But that is what people do. Sometimes the treatment is more painful than the disease, but one has to undergo it. The stronger the disease, the stronger must be the treatment. And in the West this disease of "woman and gold" has become most virulent. So it requires strong injections and medicines. In the case of every disease there is a curative crisis and this is a step leading to perfect cure.

Sometimes I pray to the Lord to send the devotees misery and trials, to make them suffer and pass through hardships, so that they may come to their senses. *Māyā* is so powerful that people forget all their past sufferings and just go on in their old ways. Something is needed to remind them constantly of the Divine.

All suffering is for our training. Our instincts are to be controlled and burnt in the fire of spiritual striving. When the iron rod has become crooked it needs some hammering. Sometimes in our egotism we forget that we are delicately poised in between the hammer and the anvil. And so when the hammer falls, we suddenly wince and exclaim, "Oh what has befallen me!" In the first place, who asked you to get in there?

Suffering need not be on the material plane alone. In the case of spiritual aspirants dry periods are common when they don't feel the original spiritual fervor, when they find themselves in the "dark night." This experience can be as painful as the sufferings of a worldly man.

The Main Cause of Suffering

People very often neglect or forget God's grace. They become over-confident in their own strength and become careless. This may even lead to arrogance. There is an amusing story in our old books. Once there was a tiny mouse in the hermitage of a sage. One day a cat fell upon it. The sage took pity on it and transformed it into a cat. Then some dogs tried to tear this new cat to pieces, and so the sage changed it into a dog. The poor dog was persecuted by a leopard and so the sage transformed it into a tiger. But when it became a tiger, it wanted to kill the sage himself. Then the sage said, "All right, just be the old mouse again."

A similar thing happens in the case of spiritual aspirants too. Divine Grace is showered on them which purifies them to a certain extent and they are able to attain a certain amount of concentration and freedom. But then they become egotistic, begin to think too highly of their attainments and become careless or go to the extent of abusing and reforming the world. Then suddenly the grace is withdrawn, and they find themselves alone, facing a terrible void.

We should all bear in mind that those who really and truly follow the spiritual path are less egocentric and more selfless, kind and considerate toward others. We have to be givers and not beggars. When it comes to material things most of the people are beggars, they want so many things from others, and yet they are egotistic! The less the ego, the greater the joy and peace, and the better our work.

Do not think lightly of your spiritual blessings. You need not constantly brood over your weaknesses and past mistakes but should cultivate alertness of mind. Constant discrimination is essential even in the path of devotion. Constant alertness of mind is essential to profit by the blessings that God is showering on us. As Shri Ramakrishna has said, if you walk one step toward God, He comes to you ten steps.

Convert Suffering into Spiritual Strength

True devotees of God do not pray for wealth or material benefits. They do not even pray for the removal of suffering. What they pray for is strength to bear their sufferings. There is a fine song by Rabindranath Tagore:

> Lord, give me the strength to bear Thy standard to whom Thou hast been pleased to give it. Give me the devotion to bear the greatest pain that is unavoidable in Thy service. Thou mayest fill my heart with great pain.
> I do not even want to get rid of this gift of suffering that Thou art giving me with Thine own hands. This misery will be my crest-jewel, if with it Thou givest me also devotion to Thee. Give me work as much as Thou likest, if Thou dost not allow me to forget Thee, nor my heart to get itself lost in the entanglements of the world.
> If Thou wishes, do Thou bind me as much as Thou likest but keep my heart open to Thee. Do Thou not allow me to forget Thee on any account.[2]

And then there is the beautiful prayer of Kunti to Lord Krishna:

> O teacher of the whole world, let calamities come to us from all directions, for they enable us to have your vision which puts an end to the cycle of rebirths.[3]

Since we are going to have unpleasant experiences anyway, it is better to have them utilized for higher spiritual life. Nobody can avoid pain, suffering, and humiliation in some form or other in his life. As it is, let these goad us to a higher purpose. Let us use them as stepping-stones to the Divine life. This does not mean that we should go out of the way and seek troubles for ourselves, as some people try to do. We should court neither suffering nor pleasure but seek the Divine alone that is beyond both.

Divine Grace may not necessarily remove all our physical miseries and sorrows, but if we have the Grace, we can pass through the fiery ordeal of life successfully, burning the dross in us in the process. This increases our inner purity and spirit of surrender. Blessed are our sufferings if they bring us clearer knowledge and steadier devotion. The more I see life, the more I understand that Divine Grace does not necessarily mean removal of our troubles. But it always gives the devotee a wonderful inner poise and strength to face all trials and difficulties, makes him purer, and enables him to feel the Divine Presence which brings an inner peace even in the midst of the greatest sufferings. Real peace is not like sleep. It is a calm state of mind that enables you to remain unmoved in the midst of the troubles and difficulties and be in touch with a vaster Reality. People who run away from the difficulties of life weaken themselves more and more. People who constantly seek pleasure and avoid their duties remain stunted. They never attain their full spiritual stature and are unable to utilize the grace that the Lord is ever ready to shower on them.

Let us make the best use of the Grace that is already showered on us. Let us make the best use of the time and advantages that we have got instead of complaining about lack of time and disadvantages and, in a spirit of surrender, let us strive for God-realization. We should strive for more Divine Grace and more love for the Divine than for the paltry things of the world which only tend to make us forget God and our spiritual destiny. We should always be in a mood to rush towards God. ...

Some Practical Suggestions

Do not make a blueprint of your life. That does not mean you should not prepare a general plan. Plan your future course in a general way, but then leave everything to the Lord. Let Him make you do what He likes.

Let us wish strongly for spiritual progress and spiritual experience. But let us leave the details to the Divine. As we do not always see things clearly, we cannot but think about our future and make plans. But all these are to be ultimately left to the Divine. We should gradually learn to be in tune with the Divine and follow the Divine Will. If we sincerely persist in this, we will come to a stage when our whole being will be in tune with the Divine.

Remember this, if one practices complete self-surrender, one cannot take any wrong step. People often glibly say, "I have left everything to God," and then they go and do as they please. One who is attached to the objects of the world or to his own desires and prejudices cannot think of self-surrender. We should always note that without a certain minimum of detachment, self-surrender is impossible. For complete self-surrender, complete detachment is necessary.

One who is poor should not wish for more than is necessary. One who is rich should replace the sense of possession with that of trusteeship, and then make the best use of what the Divine gives to one. This is true not only of material possessions, but also of intellectual resources and even spiritual blessings. Whatever you have—musical talent, efficiency in work, intellectual ideas, love—everything must be considered as a gift from God to be passed on to others. You know the story of Job in the Old Testament. He lost everything he had, but only said: "The Lord gave, and the Lord hath taken away; blessed be the name of the Lord!"⁴ We should give to deserving people whatever we can. But we should exercise great care even in making gifts, whatever they may be. Do not give things away indiscriminately in the name of self-surrender. The true devotee gets the right direction at the right time about how, when, and to whom gifts are to be given.

You need not worry so much about attaining calmness just now. There are two types of calmness: egocentric and cosmocentric. Some people appear to be calm because of their lack of love or sympathy for others. They are not bothered about other people's sufferings, and appear to be balanced and strong. But they collapse when something happens to them. It is better not to have this type of calmness. The cosmo-centric calmness comes as a result of self-surrender to the Divine, by coming in touch with Him. Only when we are established in the Universal Consciousness can we attain real calmness and balance under all circumstances.

Do not weaken yourself by being too self-critical. People go on complaining about their life because they allow the causes of their complaints to continue. Unless we make an inner change, unless we overhaul our mind, it will go on giving troubles to us. Do you know Shri Ramakrishna's parable of the pet dog? A dog had been so much fondled in the beginning that it had made a habit of jumping on to its master's body. Later on, the master wanted to control this, but the dog would not obey. Even when it was beaten it tried to jump on to the master's body.[5] Our mind is like that dog. It has been pampered so long that it is difficult to control it and surrender it at the feet of the Lord. But through repeated practice we have got to make the mind surrender itself to God.

First of all bring about a transformation in your own life, at least to some extent, through regular *sādhanā*, and then take up the ideal of "work and worship." Only you should see that you do not take up more work than you can joyfully do. In the beginning it is not possible to maintain constant remembrance of the Lord. So, offer all that you do to Him at the beginning and at the end of the work and, if possible, while you are engaged in work.

Work becomes mechanical only when you forget the goal of

your life, when you forget that whatever you do is a means to realizing God. It is no use working like a machine. The trouble with our work is not so much with the quantity of work as with its quality, that is, the way we do it. It is our inability to do our work in a spirit of dedication to God that is the main obstacle to doing work as a spiritual discipline. And there can never be any dedication unless the goal of God-realization is constantly kept in view.

Obedience to superiors is a test of our surrender to God. But the person who says that in obeying his superiors he has to sacrifice everything including his spiritual aspiration and practice, has not understood the spirit of surrender. As we practice self-surrender to God, our ego is not so much destroyed as transmuted. The individual consciousness expands and finds a place for everybody within it—superiors, juniors, and equals. True self-surrender endows a person with a higher wisdom and dignity that prevents other people from taking advantage of him.

Self-surrender does not mean you have to behave like fools. Once upon a time there was a great scholar. His wife had to go somewhere one day and she asked him to boil lentils on the stove before she returned. Now, as the cooking proceeded, the lentils started frothing up and the soup started spilling out of the vessel. The scholar immediately began to pray to God. His wife came later on, saw the mess the man had created, and asked him what he had done. She then scolded him: "You fool, could you not pour a little oil on the lentils?" When we pray to God we should pray for the wisdom to distinguish truth from falsehood, the good from the bad, the right from the wrong. Let us work as best we can with the understanding which He has already given us, and as we proceed He will fill us more and more.

It is a great bondage to depend too much on outside help and seek advice from others too often. The more you turn to the inner Guide the more free you become. Have infinite trust in the Divine and go on with the duties of your life heroically. Let the hands be busy with work and the mind occupied with thoughts of the Divine. If you have to do intellectual work and keep your mind engaged in worldly thoughts, then fix your heart, the will, on the Lord firmly. Surrender your ego to the Divine.

Transforming Work into Worship

Work and worship must go hand in hand. Our ideal is to transmute work also into worship, but it can be realized only through constant practice in the course of time. In order to succeed in this, you have to maintain something of the prayerful and meditative mood while doing your work. It does not matter if you do not succeed always. Let these failures be stepping-stones to success. With a part of the mind we have to think of the Lord while with the other part we have to attend to the duties of life, noticing of course what we are doing, and offering the fruits of the work to the Divine. All this is no doubt difficult. But let us try again and again.

Don't you know Shri Ramakrishna's parable of the woman who prepares flattened rice? With one hand she has to turn the grain in the machine, with the other she has to nurse her baby, all the while talking to friends and bargaining with customers.[6] Something of that dexterity must be brought into our spiritual striving.

You know the well-known song of Shankara wherein he says: "Whatever I do, O Lord, is Thy worship."[7] This attitude is easy when you love work. If you really dislike the work you have got to do because of some intrinsic defect in it, then please tell the Lord about your difficulties and about the fact that you are doing it only because of the pressure of circumstances. If you so wish, you may request Him to take it away from you and give something better. He will surely fulfil your wish if it is for your own good. Otherwise, you should know that it is good for you to continue with the old work in which case you may find unexpected benefits from the very work that you disliked.

I am not quite sure if Shri Ramakrishna gives us blows. Our

troubles and tribulations are the results of the working out of our *karma*. So, instead of blaming the Lord, let us profit by our experiences, however bitter they are, get dispassion more and more, and hold on to the Lord always. He is not only witnessing our trials but also is ready to help us out of them. The Lord has brought you into close contact with His spiritual current. Follow that current and maintain the contact. In due course you will feel the Divine Presence always within you, whether you sit quiet or work hard.

Work and worship must go hand in hand. And work done in the right spirit is acceptable to the Divine as much as devoted worship consisting of prayer, meditation, and so on. My teacher Swami Brahmananda gave me this instruction: "Before you begin to work remember the Lord and offer salutation to Him. Do the same at intervals in the course of the work, and also after you finish it."

Divine Grace may not necessarily remove all our physical miseries and sorrows, but if we have the grace we will be able to pass through the fiery ordeal of life successfully, burning the dross in us and attaining inner purity, and also develop greater resignation to the Divine Will. Blessed are our sufferings, then, if they bring us clearer knowledge and steadier devotion.

Take the Divine Name, think of the indwelling Spirit, feel the holy Presence, surrendering your will to His, and be at peace. Pray to the Lord for bringing new light and strength to your mind and heart. What else can you do but take things as they are and try to do your best? Whether you know it or not, your past, present, and future rest with the Lord. The best course for us is to play our part as well as we can and surrender ourselves to Him as much as possible.

Everyone has to pass through periods of great uncertainty. Whenever you feel anxious for some reason or other, repeat the Name of the Lord, think of Him and practice self-surrender. I am sure this method will bring you great strength and peace in due course.

It is only a joy to serve the Lord's cause. I am not worried about the future since I know that the past, the present, and the future rest in Him. The best thing we can do is to remember Him and surrender ourselves to Him and be absorbed in His infinite Presence, Love, and Bliss.

Offer all the fruits of your labor to Him who dwells in your heart and guides your destiny, and be at peace. Even if you think that the whole world has forsaken you, know for certain that the Lord is there with you and within you. So, pray to the Divine Lord to come to your aid, and enlighten your path. In the midst of the loneliness of your life, go on praying to Him for light and guidance and try to feel His Divine Presence even in the midst of trials and difficulties. The Lord will grant you all the strength and courage you need.

If you wish to have peace of mind, do not expect anything from anyone. If you get something, be thankful; if not, thank God. And know in your heart of hearts that the Lord alone is your own: As the Soul of your soul, He cannot leave you, nor you, Him.

Success in an undertaking does not just depend on our endeavor alone; there are also other factors that combine to make success possible. However, even when our efforts end in an objective failure, there will be a subjective success if we have worked hard in the proper spirit. Having His eye on this inner success, Lord Krishna has said: "To work alone you have the right but not to the fruits thereof."[8]

The great task in spiritual life, as in all other walks of life, is to know where we stand in relation to the Reality and face the problems boldly. Along with that, we must try to improve ourselves. If we can bring about a change for the better in the environment, well and good; otherwise we have to play our parts as best we can in the restricted situation in which we are placed.

It is sheer cowardice to try to run away from life and think of taking shelter in death. It is like falling from the frying pan into the fire and no sane person should think of it. The great disciples of Shri Ramakrishna have taught us that the spiritual seeker should not be just an automaton, always eager to be guided by someone else. We must learn to acquire conscious control over our personality, and through service, prayer, and self-surrender try to be in tune with the Divine Will and follow its bidding with devotion and steadfastness.

I have known there is such a thing as the Divine Will which works through the human will for one's own good and that of others. Through prayer, *japa*, meditation and *pūjā*, we have to contact that.

Strive to your utmost by following your higher moral sense, by fulfilling your duties in a spirit of detachment and worship, and by doing your spiritual practice with regularity and devotion. All those who have come under the influence of the Divine Power, manifest in this age in Shri Ramakrishna and the Holy Mother, are fortunate. As you unfurl your sail, you will catch more and more of the breeze of Divine Grace that is constantly blowing.

You know the analogy of the salt doll that wanted to fathom the depth of the ocean and got dissolved. It happens only in the case of the doll of pure salt, but not of the doll of sand or of the doll made of plenty of salt and sand. In all of us both "salt" and "sand" are there. In order to practice absolute self-surrender, the "sand" is to be eliminated or transformed into "salt." Our ego, with its pride and innumerable desires, cannot be transmuted easily, but attempts are to be made little by little so that eventually the "sand" is removed. Until then, we have to be like the baby monkey clinging to its mother, and follow the instruction of Lord Krishna, "Remember Me and fight the battle of life."

When the "salt" nature asserts itself, a great surge of love overpowers us and self-surrender becomes easy for the time being. But then, may be immediately afterwards, the "sand" nature which is predominant becomes strong and complete self-surrender becomes an impossibility. At that time we should not worry, but should try to remain calm.

Along with our egocentric activity, we should try to surrender as much as we can to the Divine Will. In each one of us double, sometimes triple, personalities exist, and these create no end of conflicts. One nature wages war against another and makes the confusion worse confounded.

Instead of allowing ourselves to be completely upset, we have to practice *japa* and meditation, remembering the Lord even when we are actively engaged in our duties, and offering the fruits of all our labors to Him.

The practice of self-surrender passes through three stages:

1. Whether it is spiritual practice or performance of duties, at first we do them in an egocentric way.

2. Next we learn to offer the fruits of our work to the Divine Spirit.

3. In the last stage we perform everything for pleasing the Lord. As our mind becomes purer, we feel the Divine Presence and it is only then that we feel the Lord is like the operator and we are like machines.

FOOTNOTES:

[1] *Bhagavad Gītā*, 18:61-63.
[2] Rabindranath Tagore in *Naivedya*, 20
[3] *Śrīmad Bhāgavatam* 1:8.25.
[4] *The Bible*, Job, 1:21.
[5] *Tales and Parables of Shri Ramakrishna*, p. 237.
[6] *The Gospel of Shri Ramakrishna*, p. 314-15, 380-81.
[7] *Śiva-mānasa-pūja*, 4.
[8] *Bhagavad Gītā*, 2:47.

XIV

What Personal Life?

by Rev. Michael Beckwith

We don't really have a personal life apart from God. What we call our life is actually the presence of God personified as us. The illusion of a separate life causes a tremendous amount of pain, frustration, discomfort, and disease in our life. The belief that a personal life exists apart from God creates experience disconnected from God. This is painful and frustrating. Our spiritual work is to break down the illusion that we have a life here and that a life of God is somewhere else. All of our prayer work, our meditation work, our affirmation work—the path individuals take to grow spiritually—is primarily to break down that sense of separation from God.

It's extremely important that we do the work because without an awareness of what we are, the unique pattern of God within each individual won't be expressed. Every human being, like every flower, has a unique pattern of expression. We all have a kaleidoscope of good in us—a deeper dimension accessed through our awareness that God is expressed through us and as us. So, it's not only important, it's the only game in town. It's the reason we're here.

A rose's purpose is to grow and become strong enough to bloom. When you have matured spiritually, you bloom into an awareness of your oneness with God. Without that awareness, you are immature, regardless of how much you have attained in the world materialistically, intellectually, or emotionally.

The process can be difficult. I believe the appearance that we're separate from God leads us to think that we can control our life. In truth, because our life is the life of God, It can manage itself. But we resist letting God manifest through us because some part of us wants to stay the same. Rather than change ourselves, we want to change the world and other people. But spiritual growth is just the opposite. It's about letting go of opinion, false thought, and erroneous perceptions so this other dimension can emerge. It is about totally shifting our identity. The pain comes because the ego doesn't know the difference between annihilation and transformation. So when your point of view shifts, it feels like dying. But of course you aren't dying; for the first time you are becoming fully alive.

Jesus said something I've always loved: "I have come bearing not peace but a sword to set mother at variance against her daughter, father at variance against his son ..." I've always interpreted that to mean, "I have come to cut away your lesser identities. Before you thought of yourself simply as your mother and father's child. I have come to open you to a greater identity, to bring you to understand that there is only one father, which is God."

So the lesser part of us identifies with being the son or daughter of our human heritage, but the greater part of us is eternal. Our work is to tap into that deeper dimension and learn how to let It take over, so that Its thoughts are our thoughts, Its perception is our perception, and Its perspective is our perspective. When we do this, our thoughts, words, and actions become expressions of God's love and wisdom.

Some time ago, I co-authored a song about how people are actually asleep, dreaming they're awake. I believe the average person is sleepwalking. In their dream state they try to control their world and be comfortable. Then, when they wake up, they discover that they're literally surrounded by God's presence. They're in God's grace, and God's grace is in them. They become fully alive and vitalized—and they wonder what they were doing before.

My passion for God is a deep and abiding love in the presence of God. God is everything to me. The lights went on for me well over twenty years ago, and I've never looked back. This level of passion or, as athletes would say, "staying hungry," or "being on the edge," has not diminished over the years. In fact, it's intensified. My level of commitment and discipline is even higher now than when I started. I wake up in the morning still hungry and thirsty for truth and righteousness. I'm constantly checking that I'm available for the presence of God. Being captured by a vision for your life fuels you; it gives you a passion and energy you can't get from the world.

People often ask about my meditation and prayer time. I tell them how I meditate in the morning, in the evening and throughout the day. They think, it would take a superman to do that. And I say, "No, people who *don't* practice daily are supermen. It takes a superman to be in the world, with all its powerful anti-spiritual influences." I've lived both ways, and I'd rather take the course of daily prayer and meditation. As I constantly recommit to God's vision, something else within me does the work. I don't have to make it through life on my own limited intelligence and power. To me, it's easier to yield to the Presence, yield to God, and yield to love. I just have to get out of the way. I have to submit myself. I have to be available.

Everyone can find a personal relationship with God. It does take earnestness, discipline, and commitment. But if a person truly wants to wake up, that earnestness will yield fruit. When the scriptures say, as they do in so many different ways, that those who hunger and thirst after truth and righteousness shall be fed, I believe they're talking about how that sense of earnestness makes God real to us.

It's important to know the difference between being an aspirant and a disciple. To me, an aspirant wants the results of spiritual living without paying the price. Disciples, on the other hand, completely surrender to the earnest desire within themselves to wake up. And when people really become disciples, nothing stops them until they wake up, whether it's going to churches, synagogues, or spiritual centers; finding the right book; or seeking inspiring ideas in the media. Earnestness itself creates an atmosphere where insight will happen. Their inner voice will speak to them.

Some people choose the path of keeping themselves available to God from the beginning. Others may need it pushed on them. If they live in laziness and hope the rewards of spirituality are just going to happen, then they're enrolling in the school of pain. The prisons they create will cause anguish, which, in turn, creates the need for an earnest search. The pain will push them until their vision appears, and then the vision takes over. Even so, they have to choose to embrace the vision and leave the pain behind.

Creating a Personal Relationship

Either way, if you take your heart's earnest desire to know God, and sit down every day with that and with your favorite book, your favorite author, or your favorite tape, you will be rewarded. Your spiritual realization will become more real to you than the experience of the world. When that happens, when God becomes more real to you, you will learn to exercise the commitment and discipline to stay in God-consciousness, to keep yourself truly awake. It doesn't matter who you are: the worst criminal or the best do-gooders both have the same opportunity to create a personal relationship with the spirit of the living God.

As we grow, our perception and awareness of God changes. We may begin with an elementary view of God as an individual outside ourselves who controls us and the universe. There's an old saying that God made us in His image, and we've been trying to return the favor ever since. People often view God in a human image. This God changes His mind, gets upset, answers some prayers but not others, and loves some people but not others. But even with that limited image, if we pray sincerely, we'll eventually realize that God is changeless. He's the same all the time because He's not in time—time is in Him.

Beginning seekers, especially, need to find time for God in their life, to find the discipline to make themselves available to God. If you do this at the same time every day, it will grow into a habit, and then into a way of life. When I was a beginner, I got up every morning at seven to meditate and pray; every night before I went to bed I meditated, prayed, and read spiritual material. Eventually, the boundaries between my practice and the rest of my life broke down. I discovered that while my official meditation and prayer time ended at eight, I was still praying. When I'd meet somebody at work, the prayer was still within me. If I were about to say something that wouldn't foster friendship or love, the prayer would quiet me. After a while I realized that my life was the prayer. Instead of fitting meditation and prayer into my life, I built my life around celebrating the presence of God.

Now I perform formal prayers to augment my way of life. When I wake up, the first thing I do is say, "Thank you, God— for my life, my breath. Thank you for everything." I say, "Yes, I'm here for You. Yes, I'm available. Yes, I'm ready." Even if I don't feel like it emotionally or physically, I try to engage my yes. So, I may say yes out loud: "Yes. Yes to life. Yes to love. Yes to God. Yes to beauty. Yes to creativity, excellence, and integrity. Yes, yes, yes, yes, yes, yes, yes, yes."

I also do physical exercise, *hatha yoga*, jogging, and light weight-training. And I formally meditate and pray. I never spend less than a half-hour, but more often than not, I take an hour or more to commune with God. Then I'm into my day. I also try to do a spiritual retreat a couple of times a year where I sit in silence for three to seven days at a time.

There are many ways people experience God. Sometimes, God flows through us despite our feelings that God is separate. We sometimes feel we're not ready or worthy, so we open ourselves and God pours through us despite our foibles. In other moments, the lights are dim and we don't see as clearly. We may still intellectually know our connection with God, but God seems outside of us. Finally, in other moments we cannot tell where we begin and God ends or God's life begins and our life ends. We feel completely at one with God.

There are appropriate prayers for each level. If you feel absolutely separate from God, you may find that your prayer is one of beseeching. At another level, you may evoke a law or decree to set the flow of God in motion through you. At another point, you may feel so connected and in prayer that the *prayer* is praying *you*. You may find yourself proclaiming that God is everywhere, love is everywhere. All these prayers are appropriate.

However, prayers of beseeching generally are successful because people become so exhausted that they let go and let God in. Remember, it's essential to know that all prayer is about having a shift in perception—moving from the illusion of separation to an awareness of our Oneness with the Presence. It's about moving from three-dimensional thinking to full-dimensional awareness.

Those of us trying to live a life we are proud of still make mistakes. It's natural and human. And we have to learn how to forgive ourselves. Often, we hang onto the guilt. That's really focusing on our ego, another way of trying to control our life. We feel that God will judge us, so we say to ourselves, "I might as well do the job myself. God will see how much I'm hating myself already and will lighten up on me."

In fact, self-abuse only prevents you from opening to the grace of God that's always there. God knows and loves you completely. God is not waiting for you to get your act right before He can forgive you. The nature of God is love; knowing that will make it easier for you to return to God's grace. When you realize you made a mistake and sincerely regret it, your regret means you're willing to change your actions or your perspective so it doesn't happen again. You can embrace yourself. You become available again to God, because God is still there. You had cut off the relationship by hanging onto guilt and by thinking that God was going to punish you.

Self-forgiveness is a discipline. So often people don't feel alive unless they're experiencing emotional drama. They get caught up in feeling they are a bad person and thinking that God will punish them. At some point, as you begin to mature spiritually, it's the connection with God that lets you know you're alive.

Another important part of our spiritual journey is fellowship and group worship. Gathering with other seekers creates a field of receptivity that we can all tap into. As we come together to pray and celebrate and worship—bringing the focus of our attention on God, good, love, service, and beauty—we delve deeper into that awareness. The group energy amplifies the work.

Fellowship is very important because in our industrialized Western society, our values focus on acquiring, hoarding, greed, and competition. You begin to think that's normal because you receive recognition and status for excelling in this world. When you join with others who are trying to grow spiritually, you practice a different set of values: compassion, giving, generosity of heart, time, and support rather than competition. Joining in a group is very, very dynamic, and very important for spiritual growth.

In the materialistic world, you often drop to the lowest common denominator of the emotions, but in the spiritual community, you can often transcend your emotions. You can have an insight into reality and that changes your point of view, your emotions, and your thoughts. It's beautiful. This transcendence is why so many people in a group are carried further than they thought possible. "Wow," they say. "After the service, after we held hands, after we prayed together, I saw things differently."

Even after you've experienced the gifts of fellowship, you need to develop a strategy for staying focused and available. You must remember that your solo work is equally important.

Joining a group by itself can sometimes become a form of addiction, if you're not also doing your own work. If you're riding the coattails of someone else's spiritual leadership, but you're not doing your own spiritual work, then you become a groupie rather than someone empowered by the energy of God.

To me, the key to spiritual growth and God-consciousness is understanding that we're not in the world to look for a new belief system. Instead, we're looking for ways to awaken to our real self. We are each to become the best person we can be. The quest is not about this or that religion, this or that teacher, this or that belief. It's what we can do to know who we are, and then to express our authentic spiritual identity in our human incarnation. With that perspective, we open ourselves to a greater level of empowerment and move ourselves from being victims of external forces to being expressions of God's great love and wisdom. God is Spirit, an ineffable, all-knowing Presence that is everywhere in its fullness. Where you see words like "Him," please be aware that God is beyond gender. God *is*.

XV

Love, Grace, and Surrender

by Swami Ramdas

God is defined as love. God is eternal, so love is eternal. God is peace and therefore the peace that is synonymous with God is eternal. We get from God the eternal and everlasting life if only we offer at His feet the transitory life that we are leading. So in exchange for the transitory, we get from Him the eternal. But we don't want Him. We want to struggle for so many things of the world, and depend upon them for happiness and peace, while God who is infinite joy and peace ever resides in us. What we have to offer Him is only the perishable in order to get in exchange the imperishable. God says, "Offer yourself to Me, I will give you eternal joy and peace." This dedication of ourselves to Him and doing things in His name, can be possible only by His grace.

Then, naturally, the question arises why we should have to strive for anything at all. Why should we make any effort, when grace is everything? We have to strive in order to know that by striving we do not get anything, but only by His grace. There are many who are practicing severe austerities, fasts, and so on. But they find they have not got Him. This is because His grace has not come to them. Only if you put down your pride and ego-sense, you will have Him. As long as the ego-sense persists, there is no hope. Let the ego struggle until it becomes helpless and surrenders itself to the will of God. Then His power and glory will be revealed to you. So God's help comes when we surrender ourselves entirely to Him. His grace alone can transform us. His grace alone can change the course of our life and make us struggle to achieve Him. And as we struggle on, our ego-sense gradually diminishes, until we realize our helplessness and surrender ourselves completely to Him. Our life is like a river. It should go and join the ocean, and having joined the ocean, still continue to flow towards it. We should as quickly as possible unite with the infinite ocean of Divine Existence.

The Power of Grace

The power of Grace is wonderful. In India there were great saints who by their contact had redeemed many fallen souls—those who were living a life of vice. They were saved by the touch of these saints and, sometimes, by the mere sight of these saints. The great saints pour on us their power for our inward illumination through sight, thought, or touch. If they think well of us, we are elevated. Look at the way that Jesus redeemed many of his disciples. He had twelve disciples who were fishermen, but they later became fishers of men. So contact the holy men, those who have realized God, those who live, move and have their being in the universal Spirit. They may come to us, or we may go to them. They are the saviors of the world. They are so humble, pure, kind and forgiving. They redeem even people who persecute them. Look at the power of forgiveness. By our contact with them, we grow into their likeness.

Often the example is given of a sandalwood tree that is common in India. It grows in the forest and it is said that in course of time the trees that grow near also turn into sandalwood by the breeze that blows from it. The nature of the sandalwood tree is such that, even if a man goes to it with a hatchet and cuts it, it gives only fragrance in return. Similarly, even to the persecutors, saints give only kindness, mercy, and final redemption. This is the nature of saints. The very contact of such saints proves to be surely helpful in our progress towards attaining inner purity and all that is necessary for the God-vision, which is the quest of our life. The quest of our life is eternal peace and eternal freedom that we can find only in God and nowhere else. Name, power, position, and all other worldly attainments cannot grant us this peace.

Everything is possible by God's grace. If we only have a keen desire to realize Him, He will make the path easy for us. He will provide us with all the facilities necessary and finally enable us to realize Him. There is a story in this connection.

There was a poor man in a country. He was very anxious that his king should visit him one day. But his condition was so poor that he could not make the necessary arrangements to receive the royal guest. However, he expressed his wish to the king who at once agreed to visit him. The king knew that the man lived in a very small cottage. So he sent in advance everything that was necessary for his reception at the cottage. Royal messengers went with all the things and asked the man to make use of them and also helped him in finalizing the arrangements. They got the house cleaned, spread the carpet, arranged the furniture, made the necessary decorations, and brought flowers, garlands and so on. When everything was ready, the king paid his visit. Thus the man's wish was fulfilled.

So also, if we invite God to take His seat in us, He will do everything necessary. He will Himself purify our hearts and take His seat there. So the only thing we have to do is to pray to Him to come to us. Nothing more. He will see to everything else. If your heart is sincere, you will feel the need for His coming and He will surely come to you. If your life is disorderly, He will see that it is set right and when He comes to you once, your life becomes blessed.

All are Prodigal Sons

God is all love and compassion. Ramdas can never believe He could punish us. If we are punished it is because of our own actions. If that is not the case, if He were to judge us according to our merit, He will have to reject us till eternity, for there is no end to our wrong actions and we shall never be eligible to approach Him. But how does He look at us? He looks at us with all love and compassion as a mother looks at her child. The mother does not care for any number of defects that the child may have. She does not take notice of them. God is far more loving than a human mother is. His mercy is so glorious and His forgiving nature is indescribable. We have heard the story in the Bible of the prodigal son. We are all prodigal sons. Look at the way He forgives all our sins and accepts us. He does it by His grace. He must draw us towards Him. Otherwise we cannot go to Him, we cannot even think of Him.

Thus the mystery of grace is very difficult to explain. We have seen the very worst of criminals purified in no time by Him and given His vision. In ancient India there was a robber. He used to rob people passing in front of his hut in a forest and sometimes he even killed them. Once a saint was passing that way singing God's name to himself with the accompaniment of a musical instrument. The robber ran towards him and caught hold of the instrument. The saint asked him, "What is it that you are doing?" The robber replied: "I am doing the right thing for me." The saint told him that he was committing a very grave sin by robbing people and killing them. But the robber argued that it was no sin at all, because what he did was only for the maintenance of his family. Then the saint said: "No, you are wrong. You will have to suffer for whatever sins you commit. Go and ask your wife and children if they are prepared to share your sins."

The robber quietly went home and asked his wife and children if they were prepared to share his sins. They refused to do so. Now the robber's eyes were opened and he realized that he alone had to suffer for all the sins he committed. He returned and fell at the feet of the saint and begged of him to show him the way of redemption from sins. The saint advised him to remember God and repeat His name. Thus the saint's grace came to the robber who thereafter gave up all his evil ways, took to repetition of God's name given by the saint and his life was completely transformed. He is now known as Valmiki, one of the greatest saints of India.

This is only one instance, but there are thousands of others. When grace comes to us and we start remembering God, we wonder whether we deserve the Grace at all. We cannot be sufficiently grateful to God. In what way can we express our gratitude to Him? We can only glorify Him, think of His greatness and power. His power, mercy and forgiving nature and unbounded love for us are beyond description. If we think of His qualities we simply go into ecstasy. This itself will do to purify our mind.

Today when this subject of Divine Grace was chosen by God for him, Ramdas was at his wit's end as to what to talk. For whatever he can talk about Grace will be inadequate. He cannot find words to express the mystery of Grace, still he struggles to find the appropriate words to tell you what Grace can do for us. If those who had seen Ramdas before Grace came to him are now with him, they can say what difference there is between his two lives. It is a wonderful transformation, and Grace alone was responsible for it. Ramdas can talk in praise of Divine grace for hours together, and still he will not be satisfied because Grace has made him what he is now, a humble servant of God and a confiding child of His. He goes about from place to place only to talk about Him. He has come so far from India, travelling over 12,000 miles. It is a great joy for him to talk about God and His grace. However much he glorifies Him, it is not enough. Such a God is dwelling in the hearts of you all. May He shower His grace on you and fully illumine you with His light, power, love and joy!

There is none in the world so dear to us as God. We unnecessarily cling to so many perishable things and call them ours. But we do not realize that when we were born we brought nothing with us and that when we depart from this world, we are not going to take anything with us. God alone is our eternal father, mother, and friend. Our relationship is with Him. All other things are passing. Let us play the game of life in a straightforward and honest way. Let us do everything in a state of surrender to Him and give our life in complete dedication to Him, and be helpful to our fellow beings. Service of humanity is service of God. There are several ways in which we can help our fellow beings. We can give them food when they are hungry, clothe them when they are naked, give them education when they are ignorant, and give them the touch of the Divine by ourselves living that life and awakening in them the desire and longing for God. These are the many ways in which we can serve people. We must love them in spite of their weaknesses and frailties. When Grace descends upon all in the world, their weaknesses will automatically go.

Jesus has rightly said, "Forgive them, Oh Lord, because they do not know what they do!" Look at the large-heartedness of this great Savior. He knew his persecutors did not know what they did and there was no reason why they should be hated or disliked. They did things through ignorance and ignorance was no crime. You must be compassionate, kind and sympathetic towards all, and try to lead them on the right path that leads to God. A saint was once praying to God saying: "Oh God, let me not see any fault in anybody." The moment you see fault in others, your mind becomes impure. The innocent heart does not see faults. The saints give out love to all alike. They do not see any faults in others because they see the Divine in all.

Faith and Grace

Q: Does one believe in God by his own will or by the will of God?

Ramdas: That is a question that has arisen in the hearts of millions. Faith first or Grace first? It has been conclusively told by saints who have had the highest spiritual experience that

Grace comes first. The devotee says: "Oh God, I remember You because You remembered me first." Without His grace our mind will not turn towards Him. We do not even have faith in the existence of God, unless we are awakened from within. When He awakens our sleeping soul, our mind will turn towards Him. Then we have faith in Him and we pray to Him. Otherwise we shall deny His existence. God must give us faith. That is the only way. That is how Ramdas felt thirty-four years ago. At that time he had no faith in God. But later on faith came to him because of His grace. Faith was established through experience. As Ramdas went on communing with God, he felt His presence more and more and he was convinced that God existed. Faith must gradually grow and fructify in our absorption in Him. That experience develops into His consciousness and we always feel His presence everywhere. Then we never miss Him. So faith must come through His grace. He must awaken us. We are sleeping with regard to Him. So He must wake us up and say: "I exist. Wake up and find Me."

Q: Are there different standards of morality between those who have attained God and those who have not?

Ramdas: The standard of morality must be the same all over the world. Those who have no faith in God, and therefore do not walk on the path of God, have each one a different standard of morality for himself. But those who walk on the God-path have a common standard of morality. The immoral man is he who feels he is separate from God and therefore separate from the rest of humanity. He who identifies himself with God, and so with the whole of humanity, loves all beings and does no harm to anybody. That is the standard of morality obtained in all religions of the world. It is not merely a law as you find in the Bible; here there are Ten Commandments. These Commandments will naturally be observed if you love one another. Love is the basis, guide, and inspirer. Love and God are one. So God is your inner guide. Your standard is God and none else. This is true of all religions. When God speaks through you and God's will prevails in you, you can never do wrong. You are strictly moral in the true sense of the term. Others are making rules and laws, one law for one society. They make social laws and political laws. These are all conventional things. The real law that should guide us is the law of Love. We should never do injustice and never do any selfish action at the expense of others. We will never do so if love is our guide. A man who loves will never tell lies and he will never engage himself in any dishonest activities. He will be incapable of doing anything out of selfishness, if his love is the real love which is the love of the Self or God, and not of the body.

Jesus said, "Love thy neighbor as thyself." Thyself means the immortal Self who is within you and within all. When we have this knowledge, we will be able to love all alike. This is, indeed a wonderful saying of Jesus. Lord Krishna said in the *Bhagavad Gītā*: "See Me in everything and as everybody. Love Me in everybody." It comes to the same thing. Buddha says: "Give love for hate." When people hate you, give them love in return. So all the great teachers have told us that love is the one thing that should enter into our lives, purify us, enlighten us and fill us through and through with Divine peace and joy. Where love is, there joy is. Where love is not, there the heart is dry and there is no peace. So God has been defined as both love and joy.

Q: Is there no positive value in struggle?

Ramdas: Struggle is a sure condition of progress. If you want to progress you must struggle. Otherwise life is stagnant. Stagnation is not a desirable state. Through struggle we develop strength. If you hang a bicycle on a beam and move the pedals you cannot move the bicycle though the wheel might be going round and round. You put it on the floor, sit on it, and if you push the pedal the cycle moves. Why? Because the earth offers resistance. So also struggle to overcome resistance is absolutely necessary for our onward progress.

Q: Would love not illuminate spiritual struggle?

Ramdas: Love is the end of the struggle. When you have got

122

love, your struggle ceases. The struggle is to get rid of the ego, which obstructs our getting that love which is our aim. Just as you churn curds only until you get butter you have to struggle only till you get love. ...

Surrender

Q: What is surrender?

Ramdas: You try to get Him in so many ways, but you find you remain where you were without making any progress at all, and your mind remains as bad as ever. It has thoughts it ought not to entertain. You ultimately realize that your struggle was not of any avail. You now find you are absolutely helpless and then you surrender yourself to God. He becomes your liberator.

Q: Please explain to me something more about surrender. We leave everything to God and we do nothing. Is that what you mean?

Ramdas: Yes. You do nothing. He will do everything for you. A child leaves everything in the hands of the mother and does not have any thought about the future. So mother looks after the child in every way. In the same way, if you leave everything in the hands of God, you are perfectly safe.

Q: You have to act and how are you to act then?

Ramdas: He will make you act.

Q: What am I to do then?

Ramdas: Simply wait on Him, and you will know He is in you, and you will come to feel in that state that He is the doer and not you.

Q: What are the successive stages of surrender?

Ramdas: Surrender comes through constant remembrance of God and through constant meditation on God. When you are remembering God ceaselessly, there is no room for the ego-sense to be in you. The ego-sense is clean wiped off. The moment you forget God, it is there. If you switch on the electric light, the whole room is flooded with light. But if you switch it off, there is darkness. You must switch on to Him continuously and then there will be no darkness. If there is a break in your contact with Him, at once darkness, that is, ego-sense, appears. What is needed is continuous remembrance of God. Even when we are active, doing many things in the world, we must remember God continuously and dedicate all our actions to Him. Dedication of our actions means that we must be conscious that by His power alone we are acting. There is only one power that is active in every one of us and that is God.

In our body, blood circulation is going on, various organs are active, the hair is growing. Do you think we are doing all these things? We do not do these things ourselves. What makes the sun shine? And what makes the wind blow? It is the one Power that pervades the whole universe that is responsible for all activities and movements in the universe. If we recognize and realize this truth, where is the place for the ego-sense? We have now attained a state of complete surrender.

Q: Where do the evil forces come from?

Ramdas: They are our own making. Somehow we conceive of the evil forces and they are there. In fact there is only one force and that is Divine force. We stand separate from that force and we get hits. If we attune ourselves to that force it becomes beneficent to us.

Q: If God knows everything, why do we have to ask Him? Why does He not just let us know?

Ramdas: He teaches us, but we do not want to learn. We shut ourselves from His influence. So we alone are at fault.

Awareness is Everything

Q: Is it not possible that everything we want is already here and it is only awareness that is needed?

Ramdas: Yes. There is everything here. Only our awareness is wanted. We must constantly remember Him to develop that awareness. Through remembrance alone forgetfulness goes. By bringing in light, darkness goes. If we feel one with the universal light and universal existence, our riddle is solved. We are searching for happiness outside and not within us. We think our happiness lies in possessing wealth, name, and fame; all to be got from outside. But we do not get real happiness that way. True happiness is within us, in God within us. If we find Him, we are perfectly happy. Whether we have worldly success or failure, praise or blame, our internal state is perfectly at rest.

Q: Is God going to destroy man or man is going to destroy himself?

Ramdas: Man is going to destroy himself. God is never going to destroy us.

Q: Is there a personal God-idea in the Indian philosophy?

Ramdas: There is impersonal as well as personal.

Q: Vedanta does not have any personal idea of God.

Ramdas: The great *Avatāra* who came to help mankind were all personal aspects of God. They were Rama, Krishna, Buddha, Jesus, and others. Just as Jesus is looked upon as God by Christians; Rama, Krishna and others are looked upon as God by the Hindus. They are both personal and impersonal. The impersonal Spirit has manifested as a personal being.

Q: Is a personal idea not limiting God?

Ramdas: Not at all. Limited, and still He remains unlimited. It is a wonderful combination. The infinite is appearing as finite.

Q: If there is a beginning for all things, where is the beginning for God?

Ramdas: God is eternal and there is no beginning or end for Him.

XVI

Mira: God's Love Personified

by Swami Budhananda

There is a small but tremendous word in the English language which in its all–pervasive import spans the meaning of life. It is understood and cherished by all people everywhere in the world, whatever may be their stage of evolution in the scale of civilization, or in the intricate domain of carnal passions and human sentiments. It is the motive power that moves both the sinner and the saint and is the cause of suffering and joy, comedy and tragedy, bondage and liberation.

That word is "Love." Everybody—of any age, any nation, any color, any politics, any religion or no religion—talks of love. Everybody seeks to love and to be loved. Even God is not excluded from this. Those who know God from personal experience have said that God's soul-hunger is infinitely more intense than the soul's God-hunger.

Jalaluddin Rumi, the great Sufi mystic, gives us the feel of this truth when he says:

> When in this heart the lightning spark of love arises, be sure this love is reciprocated in that heart. When the love of God arises in the heart, without doubt God also feels love for thee.

In his powerful poem *The Hound of Heaven*, Francis Thompson speaks of this quest of God for man's soul:

> I fled Him down the nights and down the days. I fled Him down the arches of the years; I fled Him down the labyrinthine ways of my own mind.

But with all his racing speed and skill of evasion, he could not escape "from those strong feet that followed and followed after."

Meister Eckhart says beautifully:

Earth cannot escape the sky; let it flee up or down, the sky flows into it, and makes it fruitful whether it will or not. So God does to man. He who will escape Him only runs to His bosom; for all corners are open to Him.

The Birth of Love

Now, how did this extraordinary love affair, which in its unimaginable sweep involves not only the entire creation but also the creator, begin? In the *Bṛhadāraṇyaka Upaniṣad* we read:

In the beginning this universe was the Self alone in the shape of a person. He reflected and saw nothing else but His Self... He was not at all happy. Therefore, a person is not happy when alone. (1:4.3)

He desired a mate. He became the size of man and wife in close embrace. He divided the body into two. From that arose *Pati* and *Patnī*, husband and wife. There (as Yajnavalkya said) the body (before one accepts a wife) is one half of oneself, like the half of the split pea. Therefore, this space is indeed filled by the wife. He was united with her. From that union human beings were born.

In whatever light we may take the statement in the Upanishads what we are expected to understand is that love is *ūrdhvamūlam*, it is, as it were, a creeper with roots in heaven. The source of love is the ultimate reality. It flows from God to creation.

Again when this love is manifested in creation, in whatever form it may appear, in the ultimate analysis, it is a movement from the created to the Creator.

There are loves and loves. Loves covered with mud and filth, lost in sensuality; and love crystal and iridescent, rising heavenward like a golden flame on wings of supersensuous flight, arousing ecstasy in God's own heart. No love is so fallen as will be completely bereft of the hidden touch of the divine. The reason for this is explained in those famous passages of the *Bṛhadāraṇyaka Upaniṣad*:

> Verily not for the sake of the husband, my dear, is the husband loved, but he is loved for the sake of the Self, (which in its true nature is one with the Supreme Self.) Verily, not for the sake of the wife, my dear, is the wife loved, but she is loved for the sake of the Self. Verily, not for the sake of the sons, my dear, are the sons loved, but they are loved for the sake of the Self. Verily, not for the sake of the wealth, my dear, is wealth loved, but it is loved for the sake of the Self.

Thus continuing, Yajnavalkya, the great seer, instructs his wife Maitreyi that nothing in this world is loved for its own sake but for the sake of the *Ātman* or the Self. With this instrument of love God's creation is perpetuated, and souls are kept bound. The greatest use, however, that can be made of love is to take it back to its source, which is God, and capture God Himself with the instrument of love.

All other loves only increase your hunger and you become sometimes morose and sometimes frustrated. As Shri Sharadamani Devi says, "The heart's innermost love should be given only to God. From all other loves comes affliction. It is only the love for God that can assuage the insatiable hunger and thirst of our souls for all time, for God is the very source of love."

Facets of Love

This all-powerful instrument of love has been used by aspirants down the centuries to realize God. The devotional scriptures have used love in five different *bhāva* or attitudes:

Śānta, the serene attitude of the seers of olden times. A quiet-flowing love, like the single-minded devotion of a wife to her husband.

Dāsya, the attitude of the servant to the master, like that of Hanuman to Lord Rama, as one finds in the *Rāmāyaṇa*, the great Hindu epic.

Sākhya, the attitude of friendship—"Come here and sit, and share this fruit," which the friends of Krishna have for Him.

Vātsalya, the attitude of the mother toward her child, like the love of Yashoda for Krishna.

Mādhurya, the sweet attitude of a woman toward her paramour, or of a bride to the bridegroom.

The Highest Devotion

Of all these attitudes, in the last mentioned, the *mādhurya bhāva*, are compounded all the other four attitudes. That is to say, this attitude of love for God can be considered to be more powerful than all the others because it includes the entire gamut of love. "God as Lord is feared; God as father is revered; God as master is honored and served; God as beloved and beautiful is embraced." This union and communion of the soul with the oversoul is known in Hindu religious literature as the consummation of *mādhurya bhāva*. It has also been called "bridal mysticism." The *gopī*, or cowherd maidens in the *Śrimad Bhāgavatam*, established an ideal of supreme devotion to the Lord for all posterity to wonder at.

In the *Nārada Bhakti Sūtra* (21), it is said: Verily it is indescribable—*parā-bhakti*, the highest form of devotion to Lord Krishna—it is seen manifest in the lives of the *gopī* of Vrindavan.

This love which is steeped in erotic imagery has often been an object of criticism by those who, to say the least, did not understand what they were criticizing. It requires a highly evolved devotee to penetrate to the heart of the supreme devotion of the *gopī* and to be able to understand its pure and superior character.

Uddhava, the great devotee, says in the *Śrimad Bhāgavatam*, "I worship the *gopī* who in their infinite love for Lord Krishna renounced their all in the world, broke the unbreakable shackles of family life. I wish I were reborn in Vrindavan as a plant so that the dust of their feet may fall on my head and purify me."

"Bridal mysticism" has not been the monopoly of Hinduism. The theory of spiritual marriage in Christian mysticism is an identical concept. The key to this way of loving God was introduced in Christianity by Christ himself in his parable of the ten virgins and the bridegroom.

The idea of spiritual marriage, or the *gopī's* way of love, was successfully cultivated by mystics like St. Bernard, Jan van Ruysbroeck, St. John of the Cross, and St. Teresa. One cannot read their lives without being convinced how all-consuming was the love of the bridegroom.

The Love of Mira

Mirabai is one of the finest examples in history of this all-consuming love for God. The very utterance of the name of Mirabai fills the mind with inspirational devotion. In Mira is seen the *gopī's* devotion to Krishna, resurrected and revivified in the great spiritual tradition. Though Mira's songs are sung everywhere in India by millions of people, in temples and monasteries, wayside inns, and even in movies, we do not yet have a universally accepted version of her life. Research is going on.

Mira was born the daughter of Ratan Singh in the early 1500s at Kudki village in a *kṣatriya* family of Rajasthan. In this martial race of the desert regions, a new type of blossom was Mira, heroic, not on the battlefront, but heroic in devotion, in self-abandonment at the feet of the Lord.

When Mira was three or four she seized upon the idol of her life from whom no power on earth could separate her. One day, a venerable sage came to her father's home and stayed overnight as a guest. The sage carried an image of Giridhara for his daily worship. During his stay at Ratan Singh's house, while he was worshiping the deity, little Mira felt irresistibly attracted to the idol, and wanted to make it her own.

But the sage was not at all ready to part with the image of this chosen idol, which he had worshiped for so long. Mira threatened to fast—the power of the aggression of this small girl's love was felt. The sage, however, was ready to give away anything he had, but not the idol of his heart.

In this duel of love, Mira became victorious, for the Lord himself indicated in a dream a preference for Mira. And the sage bent sadly over the image and with trembling hands gave it to Mira, wiped his eyes, and wended his way, musing on the strange ways of the Lord.

The mysterious telepathy that transpires between the Lord and his chosen devotees is not comprehensible to us. But one can imagine Mira's great joy at the triumph of her fancy. But perhaps you cannot imagine that this image of Giridhara could become the center and sole joy of her life.

One day, after this incident, when a marriage procession was passing by their home, little Mira asked her mother most anxiously, "Mother, where is my *dūlhā* (bridegroom)?"

"Giridhara Gopala is your *dūlhā*," said her mother, pointing at the image and smiling at the innocence of the child. But the mother perhaps also remembered what little Mira had told her of a dream in which she was married to the Lord of the Universe.

Language of the Heart

However, the seriousness with which the child had taken her mother's words was revealed, to the bewilderment of many, as she grew up. The language of her heart was recorded in her song later on:

> I have none else for my husband but Giridhara Gopala on whose head shines the crown of peacock feathers. He is my husband.

When Mira was about eight her mother died, and she came to live with her grandfather who was a devout *Vaishṇava*. At her grandfather's knee Mira listened to the spiritual lores, such as the *Mahābhārata*, with rapt attention.

As far as she was concerned, Mira knew she was already married to Giridhara Gopala. But nobody else took the marriage seriously. When Mira was about 13, her father gave her in marriage to Prince Bhojraj, son of Maharana Sanga, King of Mewar, whose capital was at the city of Chittor.

Coming to live in her husband's home, Mira disappointed almost everybody. When, according to the family tradition, she was taken to the family shrine, where the Divine Mother was worshiped, Mira declared that she did not offer obeisance to anyone but Giridhara. This startling defiance could not be understood by her own relatives. Was Mira insane or a bigot? To the family she appeared irreverent and arrogant.

The mind of a mystic of Mira's type does not function in an ordinary way. She was passing through a stage when to her the real and spiritual marriage with Giridhara was superceded by a somewhat unnecessary and unreal marriage with a prince, for whom she had little need or love. She was already committed to one husband, her God and her all, who was Giridhara. At this moment, she found the necessity of making obeisance to another deity like a denial of her loyalty.

How could she, whose heart was given away to one, have any worship to offer to another? Or what was the point of offering obeisance when the devotion was for someone else? Would it not be hypocrisy?

Another reason for the disappointment of the family was that Mira did not bring with her any of the usual worldly yearnings of a young bride. In Rajput families, which were specially devoted to the cultivation of *rājā*, young women were not expected to be ascetics. But Mira was totally of a different type. After marriage, her devotion to Ghiridhara increased and most of her time was spent in prayers and songs before the Lord. And she invited sages and holy men and had religious discourses with them. The family liked none of her ways.

Mira was ordered to abandon her own ways and follow the conventions of the royal household, but she would not conform. The spiritual yearning in her heart was so keen that it was difficult for her to tread the ordinary household path. So disciplines were imposed on her. Mira, however, reacted in her way, and she sang in a song:

> All the dear ones of this household are creating trouble over my association with holy men and are causing great hindrance to my worship. From childhood Mira made Giridhara Nagara her friend and beloved; this attachment shall never be broken but shall flourish.

When Mira was about 17, her husband Bhojraj passed away. In some literary works on Mira, Bhojraj is depicted as a jealous husband, who out of spite against his wife's devotion for God treated her badly. In some other works this is emphatically contradicted, and Bhojraj emerges as a somewhat melancholy figure who loved his wife dearly, but did not get adequate response, for Mira had given herself completely to the Lord.

In any case, after the passing away of her husband, a new chapter opened in Mira's life. It was certainly the most trying period of her life and most fruitful too. It is said that at this time, Mira received spiritual initiation from a sage, Raidas. Her widowhood, by itself, could only mean for her an intensification of spiritual life.

Now after receiving initiation from a spiritual teacher her spiritual yearning and absorption, her longing for holy company, her utter disregard for the conventional ways of the world—all increased a thousandfold and created difficulties for her. Meanwhile, her father-in-law Rana Sanga passed away, and Prince Vikramaditya (Vikramjit), became the Rana or king at Chittor. He wasted no time in extending disciplinary measures to Mira.

Mira's devotional practices were uniquely her own. She danced and sang before Giridhara Gopala. And she would lose no opportunity of associating with holy men. Her yearning for holy association was so great that she set aside all conventions of the royal household to get the inspiration of spiritual company. This hunger for holy company was naturally not understood by those who had not undergone self-purification.

Vikramjit passed orders that Mira should give up her unseemly singing and dancing before the image and the even more objectionable seeking of the company of holy men. Was she not a woman, a widow? Then why so much anxiety to meet with men? Vikramjit did not hesitate to spread scandal against this purest of pure woman.

When Mira was obstructed in her worship in the palace, she went to a temple outside, and there continued her spiritual practices. Her supreme devotion and ecstasies soon attracted attention, and from far and near people began to flock to her, to give homage and to receive spiritual inspiration. This angered the Rana and others in the household all the more. Mira was now virtually made a captive in the palace and one inhuman torture followed upon another.

Mira was not only a lover of God, but an inspired poet. Her poems, which she used to make song offerings to the Lord, give an account of what she had to go through at the hands of the Rana.

You will be surprised how tremendous were the oppressions, but how easily Mira went through them. In a song Mira records her experience:

> Mira is happy in the worship of her Lord; Rana made her a present of a serpent in a basket; Mira, after her ablution, and opening it found the Lord himself. Rana sent a cup of poison; Mira, after her ablution, drank the cup which the Lord had turned to nectar. Rana, sent a bed of nails for Mira to sleep on; that night when Mira slept on it, it became a bed of flowers. Mira's Lord averts all her troubles, ever her kind protector; Mira roams about in ecstasy of devotion. She is a sacrifice to the Lord.

Understanding Grace

Mysterious and various are the ways in which God's grace flows through the lives of devotees. When Bernard Shaw heard the news of Gandhiji's assassination, he exclaimed, "This is the consequence of being a good man in this world!" Gandhiji was a devotee of Shri Ramachandra. When a few days before his assassination a bomb had burst in his prayer hall, and Gandhiji escaped unscathed, people thought, "Who can destroy him whom God protects?"

Again, Prahlada, who was a boy devotee of Vishnu, could not be killed by being trampled under the foot of an elephant, or thrown from a hill top, or by being administered poison, or various other ways. Similarly Giridhara saved Mira in all possible ways.

Ordinarily we are bewildered when we study the various consequences of being a true devotee of God. Our difficulty in understanding grace arises from the fact that we have a gross view of devotion as an investment. I have loved God—so he must now become my policeman, doctor, lawyer, or a lifeboat for me wherever I am in trouble.

As a cash return for devotion, we want security bonds from heaven. This in religion is racketeering and commercialism taking the various forms of the promissory notes of "indulgences."

Thus, grace is present not only when the poison turns to nectar; it is also there when the poison works. The Lord's grace is there when the good man graciously takes the consequences of being good.

Mira took the poison not because she was in anyway sure that it would turn to nectar, but because whatever was sent came from the Beloved. The proof of grace is in this God-given capacity for ready acceptance of whatever comes from the Lord; and from the standpoint of the devotee the consequences just do not matter.

When Pavhari Baba, the great Indian saint, was smitten by a

serpent, he exclaimed, "Ah, a messenger from the Beloved!"
Good and evil, pain and pleasure, prosperity and adversity, life
and death—all are messages from the Beloved. When we do not
see this dual throng of opposites as acceptable or unacceptable,
but only as a conferring of love from the Beloved, we have
tasted *bhakti* or devotion.

The proof of God's grace is not in any incident, favorable or
unfavorable but in the God-infused strength of the soul, which
can accept anything that comes with joy and resignation. It is not
in what comes, but how you are given to receive what comes.

Vikramjit was a harsh, insensitive man, and he thought un-
dependable Mira required strict vigilance. So he appointed his
own sister Udabai—because he thought that he could not depend on others to do this delicate job faithfully—and three other
women to keep watch over her. Uda tried her best to change
Mira's mind and ways.

An interesting conversation between them has come down
to us and gives us insight into Mira's unworldly and fearless
character.

Uda: Mira, give up this company of holy men. There's scandal in the city.

Mira: Let them spread the calumny. What's that to me? I am
devoted to holy men.

U: Why don't you wear your pearl necklace and your precious jewelry?

M: I have thrown them away. Holy thought and content-
ment are my ornaments.

U: At other places one sees beautiful processions and con-
gregations of men and women, and at your place only all sorts of
devotees of God assemble.

M: Go to the terrace of the palace and see how wonderful is
the assembly of holy men.

U: All people of Chittor are ashamed of you; and the Rana
hangs his head low.

M: Chittor is free today—the way for Rana's deliverance is
also open.

U: Your parents are ashamed of you. You are the cause of stigma to your birthplace.

M: My parents are blessed. My birthplace is also blessed.

U: Rana is angry with you. And he has kept poison for you in the casket of gems.

M: That is fine. I shall drink it as the sacrificial water.

U: That is not ordinary poison. The very sight of it will kill you.

M: I have none in the world. Mother earth will accept me.

U: Ranaji wants to know what is your path and aim of your life.

M: My path is sharp as the razor's edge. Rana will not be able to reach that region.

U: Don't be disobedient to the Rana. Obey him. If he is angered there will be no shelter for you.

M: Uda, Giridharilal is my only refuge. I pray to Him with all sincerity.

But Uda failed in her attempts to convert Mira to her way of thinking. Mira lived in her own world; threats or allurements of this world had little sway over her.

However a conversion took place, not of Mira but of Udabai. The touch of the philosopher's stone burned the brass metal into gold. Vikramjit had much faith in Uda, for he thought the latter was his loyal follower. But holy company is an explosive thing.

One day, forgetful of the world, alive only in her Lord, Mira was passionately singing this song:

> Since I have met Him, my friend, I have said goodbye to all decorum and modesty; none please me—none can fetter me. Ah, the peacock crown He donned, and the beautiful mark on His forehead. Who in the three worlds can resist His charm? All succumb to His enchantment.

As Uda listened to the outpouring of Mira's soul in her song and supplication, she experienced an inner transformation and fell at Mira's feet, asking to be taken as her disciple.

This was the end of one type of vigilance and beginning of another for Uda. Her transformation was instantaneous. Pining to have the vision of Giridhara, Uda begged Mira to get her that vision. Mira was by nature large-hearted; and she was so deeply moved at Uda's yearning that her heart swelled in prayer and she begged her Lord to fulfill Uda's yearning.

Fruit of Holy Company

It was midnight. Uda and her three companions, Mithula, Champa, and Chameli, were all seated in the shrine, Mira was pouring out song after song in her celestial voice. To their utter amazement, all of a sudden Giridharalal appeared and said, "Mira, why are you so very deeply agonized tonight for me?" Such was the incredible fruit of holy company, that not only Uda but also her three companions, who had not specially craved for it, all had the vision of the Lord.

Perhaps, noticing that Uda was no longer trustworthy, Vikramjit appointed special guards to keep watch over Mira's temple day and night. At long last Mira was caught. At midnight the guard brought the news secretly to the Rana that Mira was frolicking with a person in the temple. Sword in hand, the Rana rushed to the shrine and finding no one asked Mira, "where is the man with whom you have been frolicking all this while?"

"My beloved is there standing before you. Then why do you ask me?" replied Mira.

The angry and self-righteous Rana, however, unable to see the Lord, proceeded to make a special search, when to his utter fright and dismay he saw the horrible figure of a man-lion confronting him. Valorous Rana Vikramjit swooned on the ground, sword in hand. And Mira herself was not a little surprised because the same Giridhara, who was sporting with her as the Beloved had now assumed this horrible form to frighten her tormentor.

For the Rana it was too shocking an experience. Therefore

there soon came an order from the Rana, ostensibly to save the prestige of the family, that Mira must leave Chittor. This was an order of banishment. For a lady of the royal household it was not an easy order to obey, but inside, Mira was a revolutionary and did not care what was in store for her. Was not Giridhara her beloved and her refuge?

Before leaving she sang for the Rana's household firmly and frankly.

> If the Rana is angry, what harm can he do to me? Friend, I shall continue to sing the glories of Giridhara; if the Rana is angry, his own kingdom will give me shelter; but if God is angry, my friends, where can I go? Friends, I care not to fol-low worldly conventions, and shall unfurl the banner of inde-pendence. I shall row the ship of God's name and will cross the illusory world. Friends, Mira has taken refuge with the powerful Giridhara and will cling to His feet.

Mira left Chittor, and the very Goddess of fortune was gone, as it were, from the capital. Shortly after her banishment, the waves of invasion in Chittor by Muslim chiefs began, at the conclusion of which the city was reduced almost to a mass of ruins.

For a while, Mira stayed with her uncle at Merta, but as political misfortune overtook him, Mira was compelled to leave Rajputana. Her Giridharalal had probably a fancy to see the lady of a royal family standing and singing the glories of His name on the dusty roads.

Mira was now a veritable beggar, a singing minstrel, mov-ing from one place of pilgrimage to another. In this most trying situation her dependence on the Lord increased a hundredfold, and in a ringing voice she sang her immortal song of renuncia-tion:

> Father, mother, brother, or friend, I have none. Lord, for your sake I have given up all happiness. Do not forsake me now! Do not forsake me.

On this pilgrimage, there were moments when she felt that she was forsaken by the Lord. This, in fact, was only her hunger for his perpetual vision, and so like a neophyte she would cry: "Lord, will you not grant me your vision, before life leaves this body?"

Embodiment of Devotion

Though now homeless, Mira was not, however, alone. Such was the power of her wonderful songs, steeped in devotion that crowds followed her wherever she went. The supernal beauty of her purity, the regal dignity of her person, her infinite humility, fathomless devotion, fearlessness, absolute surrender, and her transmuting songs, gave a new sort of experience, even for the people who had seen so many saints.

Such absolute love for God and absolute renunciation had never been seen before. But the outpouring of Mira's divine passion in song has such a special character that even among the melodious mystics Mira stands out as a singular saint whose very name has become an inspiration to spiritual aspirants for all time.

Nobody knows how many songs Mira sang in the privacy of her soul to her Lord. We have now some 500 on record. This is a highly valued treasure in our spiritual lore. It is impossible to sing or to hear Mira's songs without having an influx of her passion for God well up in one's heart.

Wandering in this melodious way, spreading everywhere waves of devotion and yearning for the Lord, Mira came to Vrindavan, the great place of pilgrimage for *Vaiṣaśnava*.

In his lifetime Lord Krishna's sport with the *gopī* was enacted in the sylvan surroundings of Vrindavan, and the *gopī* were the greatest devotees of Krishna, whom they worshiped in the *mādhurya bhāva*, the attitude of the beloved to the sweetheart. That was exactly the attitude of Mira to Krishna.

Some even used to hold the view that Mira had herself been a *gopī* in her previous life. You therefore can imagine her joy in being at the place where her beloved has sported, in his incarnation as Krishna. It was not all joy, however, for the constant remembrance of Krishna agonized her heart beyond description and she pined for the constant vision of the Lord.

When the devotees became aware of her extraordinary love for Krishna they began to throng around her for inspiration. Her devotional singing, or *bhajan*, attracted crowds.

Nor did Mira lose any opportunity of associating with holy men. At that time Jiva Goswami, the great disciple of Shri Chaitanya, was living in Vrindavan, Mira sought an interview with him. But the saint, a hyper-religious ascetic, refused to see Mira because she was a woman. On being refused an interview, Mira sent the sage a note that brought him new enlightenment. She wrote:

> It was surprising that the revered saint had not yet transcended the sex-idea! And that in Vrindavan, Lord Krishna alone is *Puruṣa*, all others are *prakṛti*. If the saint considers himself as *Puruṣa* and not as a *gopī*, it is better he leaves the sacred place, where Lord Krishna once sported.

The saint at once recognized that he was encountering a person of higher enlightenment and deeper realization. Without loss of time he met Mira, paid her his obeisance, and begged pardon, while Mira paid her respects to him.

Now this requires explanation: why did Mira say that Krishna was the only male principle and all others (men and women) represented the female principle? In short, this idea means that the creator God alone is the directive, operative, and active principle whereas all created beings, the *jīva* or the embodied souls, are only receptive and responsive principles.

The Creator is the source of all energy and the creation is the vessel and the manifestation of the energy. Thus, a mystic may look upon God as the only male principle and all men and women as representing the female principle. ...

From Vrindavan, after visiting Mathura and some other

141

places of pilgrimage, Mira at last came to Dvaraka and settled there for the remaining period of her life. Like Vrindavan and Mathura, Dvaraka is also a place associated with Lord Krishna's life, and He is known there by the special name of Shri Ranachhorji. At the feet of the Lord, in the temple, Mira passed her days happily singing her songs. She learnt Gujarati, composed songs in that language, and came to be adored by the local people as a saint with deep mystic experiences.

After Mira had left the palace in Chittor, Mewar went through fire. Muslim invasion brought havoc to the entire kingdom. Chittor, the capital, was in a bad state, and Vikramjit, who during his rule had banished Mira from Chittor, was no longer the king.

The new king, Udaisingha, was a God-fearing man, who realized that all their misfortunes were well-deserved, for the royal family had ill-treated saintly Mira.

He lost no time in sending the most revered priest of the capital, along with some other dependable persons, to bring back Mira to Chittor from Dvaraka. But when they came to Dvaraka, notwithstanding their continuous, piteous, and persuasive request, Mira refused to retrace her steps. She would not leave the feet of the Lord. What was Chittor to her?

At last the messenger-priest took an extreme step and threatened a hunger strike if Mira would not change her mind. This *satyāgraha* of the priest perturbed Mira, for she could not see a man dying for her sake. Helpless as she was, Mira entered the temple to take leave of Shri Ranachhorji, the deity, and in a piteous melody she sang, "Lord, you are the remover of miseries of all beings, O Giridharalal! Mira is your maidservant. Where there is misery, there also is misery's remover."

We are told that God takes seriously the prayers and supplication of souls that are pure and self-given. Mira's songs vibrated inside the temple and it would appear also inside the heart of the deity, while ceaselessly the waves of the ocean broke on the seashore outside the temple. Mira was alone inside the temple with the Lord. Her plaintive melodies poured forth. The priest-messenger was waiting outside with his followers in the joyful expectation that they would ultimately be able to return to Chittor with the goddess of their fortune.

The waves of the ocean rolled on. Time waited for none, and the door of the temple continued to stay closed. When the door was finally opened from outside, the wonder was great indeed. Mira had vanished. Shri Ranachhorji had not given her leave to go He had taken her unto Himself. Where did she or could she go? The temple was closed. The priest-messenger was sitting at the door. A thorough search inside yielded no results.

Presently the plaintive sweet voice of Mira was heard singing the refrain of her last song: "O Giridhara Nagara, O my Lord! Do not forget Mira, may she be joined with You!"

From where did the voice come? Was she hiding anywhere? Despite a search, Mira could not be found. She was not to be taken to Chittor, for she had returned to her eternal capital, the heart of the Lord. Mira, through the power of her love, had become physically resolved in the person of the deity. The proof of this was revealed by the discovery of Mira's veil on the face of the deity.

In the spiritual history of India there have been a few other cases in which the devotee became dissolved in the person of the deity.

Andal, who was born with the same ecstatic love for Shri Ranganatha as Mira had for Giridhara Gopala, and refused to marry anybody else but the Lord, got dissolved, sucked, as it were, into the image of Shri Ranganatha at Shrirangam.

Her hymns, which are some of the most inspiring devotional lyrics in Tamil literature, are sung as a part of early morning devotions, especially in the months of December and January, everywhere in the Tamil-speaking areas of South India. It is also said that Shri Chaitanya, who was a contemporary of Mira, vanished in the same mysterious way in a temple in Puri. And a similar story is told about another celebrated saint, Tukaram.

This is Mira's story, a life lived completely in search of God, with absolute and heroic unconcern for the world and worldliness. A life in which bridal love for God attained its astonishing fulfillment even as it did in the life of the *gopī*, a life from which flows an unending stream of inspiration to aspirants who tread the path of devotion to the Lord.

Mira is not just a heartbeat but the very soul-vibration of India. And why should we say "of India?" Mystics do not belong to any race. They belong to God as God belongs to them. Their true language is not just a spoken dialect but the yearning of the soul.

Now, though we have narrated here all the known facts of her life, we must confess it is beyond our power to present the real Mira. For the real Mira is not the Mira of the happenings of her life, but the Mira of the hastening soul, the Mira of agony and suffering, or bleeding heart and scorched spirit, the Mira pining and prostrated by separation from the Lord—and again the Mira of resurgence and beatitude in her union with the Lord.

If you want to have a glimpse of this real Mira, you must hear a musically gifted devotee of Lord Krishna sing her songs with self-abandon. Then you will have a small glimpse of the inner being of Mira. In her devotional songs Mira lives on. As we cannot conceive of the death of electricity, so we cannot conceive of the death of love. In *bhakti*, the devotee lives. *Bhakti* is not a one-way traffic. It is a fusion of God's breath to the soul and the soul's response to it.

XVII

Total Surrender

by Swami Tejomayananda

That which is called Self-realization in the language of knowledge is known as the state of total surrender in the language of devotion. It is a state of total annihilation of the ego. In the path of knowledge (*jñāna yoga*), the first step is to make the mind subtler by inquiry (*vicāra*), and the last step comes when one knows oneself to be the Infinite Self, when the ego is destroyed completely. In the path of devotion, however, the first step itself is surrendering of the ego at the altar of the Lord. And all efforts are to be put forth in this direction alone.

There are many aspects of surrender. It is easy to say that we have surrendered, but few of us know what true surrender is. The attitude of, "Thy will be done, not mine," truly shows surrender. When Mirabai was sent poison by her husband, she said that it was the Lord's will and drank it with joy. Subsequently the poison turned into nectar for her. That is the glory of total surrender.

On the one hand, we say that we have surrendered to God, and on the other we still hold onto our own will and ego. Both of these attitudes cannot go together. Sometimes we attribute certain things to God's will, and sometimes to our own. We should either exercise our own will, act accordingly, and own the results of our actions in a gracious manner, or totally surrender to His will.

We only say that we have surrendered our will, that we have

handed over all our responsibilities to the Lord, and that He will take care of everything, but we are not sure of it. We pray to God while we harbor doubts whether He would listen to or take care of us, and so we do not experience the result of total surrender. Therefore, it is important to know what true surrender is.

The Need for Surrender

Why do we need to seek refuge? When it rains suddenly, we run for shelter. In the scorching heat of the sun, we seek the shade of a tree. When we are suffering from a disease; we seek the help of a doctor. In financial crises, we look for support from a rich colleague. In family troubles, we seek the company of a sympathetic friend. We seek the support, help, company or refuge of another to alleviate our physical and mental sorrows and for solutions to the problems we face in life.

Naturally we should surrender to one who is capable of alleviating our sorrow. We are not going to receive financial help from a pauper when we are in a financial crisis, even though he may sympathize with our condition. We cannot surrender to one who is himself insecure or miserable. Such a person can only add to our own insecurity, or may even seek sympathy and help from us. Also, we find that a person who may give us financial help may not be able to provide psychological solace or physical security. Thus, it is best to surrender to the Lord alone, as in Him we receive support and solace for all our problems at once. As the Lord is omniscient, omnipotent, all bliss, ever present, and all love, we can attain real peace in Him alone. Tulsidasji said that surrendering unto Him, he found supreme peace.

On the battlefield of Kurukshetra, when Arjuna was not sure about the right course of action, Lord Krishna gave him the knowledge of the *Bhagavad Gītā*. After expounding various means to purify the mind and gain knowledge through *karma yoga* and *dhyāna yoga*, the Lord concluded with the famous verse: "Give up all other means, duties, paths and surrender all

146

unto Me alone. I shall free you from all sins. Rest assured do not grieve." Lord Rama also promised that if a person even once, sincerely offers himself to the Lord, He will make him fearless. Therefore, is Lord's Krishna's promise to liberate the devotee from all sins different from Lord Rama's promise to release the devotee from all fear? No, for sin causes fear, and fear causes sin, and both cause bondage and sorrow. So we see the Lord assuring us that those who surrender to Him will be free from all sorrow and bondage.

The Six Factors of Surrender

The *Vaiṣṇava sampradāya* describes the six-fold factors of surrender as: 1) Entertaining favorable thoughts. 2) Renouncing unfavorable thoughts. 3) Having firm faith that God will protect. 4) Seeking refuge in the Lord. 5) Submitting oneself completely to God's mercy. 6) Expressing one's total helplessness.

1) *Entertaining favorable thoughts.* First there must be the thought, I want the Lord and I want to reach Him. I am willing to do anything that is conducive to reaching Him. I will make myself fit for receiving His grace. I will equip my mind with the qualities that are required for gaining His vision (*darśana*). I will attend *satsaṅga*, follow the instructions of my guru, and do regular spiritual practices. I will try to please the Lord with my actions. I will serve Him in every way. To entertain such thoughts is the first aspect of surrender.

2) *Renouncing unfavorable thoughts.* In order to attain the Lord, I am willing to give up anything that is not conducive toward that endeavor. I effortlessly give up all pleasures, name, fame, power, relationships, and wealth if they prove to be obstacles in my path. I give up all objects and attachments that obstruct my spiritual progress. I give up all worldly talk of pleasures, wealth, non-believers, and the company of pleasure-loving or evil-minded people. I willingly give up false notions and prejudices, and am ready to work tirelessly to renounce anger,

jealousy, pride, hypocrisy, and other negative traits. This kind of thinking and action is the renunciation of unfavorable thoughts.

3) *Having firm faith that God will protect.* This is firm faith not only in the existence of God, but also in that He protects me at all times under every circumstance. He is not just my "wish-fulfiller" but my "well-wisher." He, therefore, does what is best for me. I may not understand or appreciate His ways, but I know that whatever happens, happens for the best, because His protective and guiding hand is behind all that I get in life. He is kind and compassionate, and His love for me is unconditional. I am His child, and He will never abandon me whatever I do. No problem is too big for Him. He will take care of me. I do not have to worry. I am protected by His blessings that He abundantly showers on me, despite what I am.

4) *Seeking refuge in the Lord.* I may have faith but I actually need to seek refuge in the Lord. I actually pray for protection, blessings, and grace. I ask for liberation, "I come to you as I am; make me what You want me to be. I have come this far, take me further. Hold me. Guide me to the Truth. You have guided me till now, help me further, bless me always."

5) *Submitting oneself completely to God's mercy.* This is falling at the feet of the Lord or surrendering totally to Him. I say, "I am Yours to do with as You please. I have no will or wish of my own. I am like the flute in Your hands. You can play whatever tune You wish to play." In submitting ourselves to the Lord, there is no longer any resistance or any reservation that obstructs total surrender. King Bali not only gave his entire kingdom to Lord Vamana but finally gave himself to the Lord. He surrendered not only his possessions (my-ness) but also his ego (I-ness). This is *ātma-nikṣepa*, also called *ātma-nivedanam* in the nine-fold aspects of Devotion propounded by Sage Narada.

6) *Expressing one's total helplessness.* As long as we think that we can do things by our own effort, independent of the Lord, *Bhagavān* does not interfere. He is very democratic. If we think we can do something, He will let us do it. But as soon as we

seek refuge, surrender unto Him, and reveal our helplessness, He responds and comes forward to uplift us.

Vibhishana, the youngest brother of Ravana from the epic *Rāmāyaṇa* was one of the greatest devotees who surrendered to Lord Rama. If his character is studied in detail one finds all the six factors of surrender in him. May we be inspired to surrender like Vibhishana and attain supreme devotion, peace, and fulfillment. Let us open our hearts to receive the highest divine grace and blessings. He showers His gifts and blessings in plenty, unconditionally, and unasked. Why not surrender completely to one so great!

About the Authors

Beckwith, Rev. Michael

Reverend Michael Beckwith is Founder and Senior Minister of the Agape International Spiritual Center, headquartered in Los Angeles, California, USA. The Agape International Spiritual Center is associated with centers in Brazil, Jamaica, and Africa. Dr. Beckwith is also National Co-Director (with Mary Manin Morrissey and Arun Gandhi) of "A Season for Nonviolence," an international movement to actualize world peace, convened by the Association for Global New Thought, sponsored by the M.K. Gandhi Institute for Nonviolence.

Daya Mata, Sri

Sri Daya Mata is the foremost living disciple of Paramahansa Yogananda. She entered Paramahansa Yogananda's ashram in Los Angeles in 1931. The great Guru's life came to a close in 1952. In 1955, Sri Daya Mata became president of Self-Realization Fellowship-Yogoda Satsanga Society of India. As spiritual successor to Parahamansa Yogananda, she sees to the guidance of SRF/YSS members, the training of monastic disciples who reside in the Self-Realization/Yogoda ashrams, and the faithful carrying out of Paramahansa Yogananda's ideals and wishes for the dissemination of his teachings and the expansion of his spiritual and humanitarian work worldwide.

Kearney, Tim

Tim Kearney taught literature and lectured on a part-time basis in the Anglo-Irish Department of University College, Dublin and at All Hallows College, Dublin for two years. He lived and worked in the L'Arche community of Trosly-Breuil from 1982 to 1984. He became Founding Director of the L'Arche community in Cork in 1984. In 1996 he became the Regional Coordinator of L'Arche in Ireland. He has worked on the editorial board of "The Crane Bag" journal, as well as "The Letters of L'Arche". He has written widely on L'Arche and on issues of contemporary spirituality and has led retreats in recent years. He and his family are members of the L'Arche community.

Jean Vanier is the son of former governor General Georges Vanier of Canada, and founder of L'Arche, an international network of communities for people with intellectual disabilities.

Khan, Hazrat Inayat

Hazrat Inayat Khan was born in Baroda on July 5th, 1882 into a musical dynasty, as his grandfather was the court musician of the Maharaja of Baroda. He traveled throughout India and became very well known as a court singer and Veena player. While traveling he studied the religious and mystical orders of India and was initiated into the Sufi orders.

Powell, Father John

Father John Powell, a Chicago native and member of the Society of Jesus, is currently a retired professor of Theology at Loyola University in Chicago. Father Powell has published 21 theological and psychological books, which have been translated into more than thirty languages.

Rinpoche, Sogyal

Sogyal Rinpoche was born in Tibet and raised by one of the most revered spiritual masters of this century, Jamyang Khyentse Chökyi Lodrö. He travels and lectures throughout the world and is the founder and spiritual director of Rigpa, an international network of Buddhist groups and centers.

ABOUT THE AUTHORS

Swami Ashokananda

Swami Ashokananda joined the Ramakrishna Order in 1921 and took the vow of *samnyāsa* in 1923 from Swami Shivananda, second President of the Order. He served as the editor of the *Prabudhha Bharata*, from 1926 to 1930. And was Swami-in-charge of the Vedanta society of Northern California, San Francisco, (founded by Swami Vivekananda in 1900) from 1932 till his passing away in December 1969 at the age of 76.

Swami Budhananda

Swami Budhananda, a guest lecturer at the Vedanta Society of Northern California, was for several years Assistant Minister of the Ramakrishna-Vivekananda Center of New York. In India he was associated for a time with the Ramakrishna Math, Chennai, as Editor of *The Vedanta Kesari*.

Swami Chinmayananda

Swami Chinmayananda, the founder of Chinmaya Mission, was a sage and visionary. He toured tirelessly all around the world giving discourses and writing commentaries on the scriptural knowledge of Vedanta, until he left his bodily form in 1993. (See write-up at the end of this book.)

Swami Pramathananda

Swami Pramathananda joined the Ramakrishna Order of monks, in 1950. After joining the Order, initially he served in educational and cultural centers in India, and was the principal of two residential schools. He also served successfully in interior Tribal areas in India. In 1982 Swamiji came to the West to serve as the Assistant Minister at the Vedanta Society of Sacramento,

California. In March 1989, he took charge of the Vedanta Society of Toronto, devoted to the study and practice of Universal philosophy and religion, where he conducts regular services and classes.

Swami Ramdas

Swami Ramdas (1884-1963) was initiated in Ram Mantram by his father. In 1922 he renounced worldly life and wandered as a *sādhu* throughout India and the Himalayas in a divine state of God-intoxication. As he himself had attained realization by taking to uninterrupted chanting of the Divine name, he always extolled the virtue of *nāma japa*. He assured all seekers that this would lead them to the heights of Self-realization. He founded an ashram in the north of Kerala with the name of "Anandashram."

Swami Shraddhananda

Swami Shraddhananda, who was head of the Vedanta Society of Sacramento from 1964 until his passing in 1996 was born in East Bengal in 1907. In 1930, at the age of 23, Swami Shraddhananda joined the Ramakrishna Order and was ordained into *saṁnyāsa* in 1939. Swamiji came to the United States in 1957. Besides having a strong love for music, Swamiji served as editor for the Bengali journal *Udhodhan* and wrote several biographies and other books.

Swami Swahananda

Swami Swahananda has been the Minister of the Vedanta Society of Southern California since 1976. He joined the Ramakrishna Order of the Vedanta Society in Calcutta in 1947. Swamiji had been a teacher at the Belur Math, the editor of the journal *The Vedanta Kesari,* and the head of the New Delhi Vedanta Center before he came to the United States.

ABOUT THE AUTHORS

Swami Tejomayananda

Swami Tejomayananda, the spiritual head of Chinmaya Mission centers worldwide since 1993, is fulfilling the vision of his guru, Swami Chinmayananda. As Mission head, Swami Tejomayananda has already conducted more than 350 *jñāna yajña* worldwide. He has served as dean or acarya of the Sandeepany Institutes of Vedanta, both in India and in California. Fluent in Hindi, Marathi and English, and lecturing and writing commentaries in all three languages he makes even the most complicated *Vedāntika* topics clear to his audience.

Swami Viprananda

Swami Viprananda of the Vedanta Society of Southern California is at the Ramakrishna Monastery, Trabuco Canyon, U.S.A.

Swami Yatiswarananda

Swami Yatiswarananda (1889-1966), a former Vice-President of the Ramakrishna Math and Ramakrishna Mission, was a well-known spiritual figure in the Neo-Vedanta movement. He spent several years spreading Vedanta in Europe and U.S.A. His *Meditation and Spiritual Life* has been acclaimed as a spiritual classic.

Pronunciation of Sanskrit Letters

a	(but)	k	(skate)	t	⌈think or	ś	(shove)
ā	(father)	kh	(Kate)	th	⌊third	ṣ	(bushel)
i	(it)	g	(gate)	d	⌈this or	s	(so)
ī	(beet)	gh	(gawk)	dh	⌊there	h	(hum)
u	(suture)	ṅ	(sing)	n	(numb)	ṁ	(nasaliza-
ū	(pool)	c	(chunk)	p	(spin)		tion of
ṛ	(rig)	ch	(match)	ph	(loophole)		preceding
ṝ	(rrrig)	j	(John)	b	(bun)		vowel)
ḷ	⌈no	jh	(jam)	bh	(rub)	ḥ	(aspira-
	⎪English	ñ	(bunch)	m	(much)		tion of
	⎨equiva-	ṭ	(tell)	y	(young)		preceding
	⌊lent	ṭh	(time)	r	(drama)		vowel)
e	(play)	ḍ	(duck)	l	(luck)		
ai	(high)	ḍh	(dumb)	v	(wile/vile)		
o	(toe)	ṇ	(under)				
au	(cow)						

Other Chinmaya Publication Series:

THE *Self-Discovery* SERIES

Meditation and Life
by Swami Chinmayananda

Self-Unfoldment
by Swami Chinmayananda

THE *Hindu Culture* SERIES

Hindu Culture: An Introduction
by Swami Tejomayananda

The Sanskrit word *Mananam* means reflection. The *Mananam Series* of books is dedicated to promoting the ageless wisdom of Vedanta, with an emphasis on the unity of all religions. Spiritual teachers from different traditions give us fresh, insightful answers to age-old questions so that we may apply them in a practical way to the dilemmas we all face in life. It is published by Chinmaya Mission West, which was founded by Swami Chinmayananda in 1975. Swami Chinmayananda pursued the spiritual path in the Himalayas, under the guidance of Swami Sivananda and Swami Tapovanam. He is credited with the awakening of India and the rest of the world to the ageless wisdom of Vedanta. He taught the logic of spirituality and emphasized that selfless work, study, and meditation are the cornerstones of spiritual practice. His legacy remains in the form of books, audio and video tapes, schools, social service projects, and Vedanta teachers who now serve their local communities all around the world.